# Creative Bible Activities for Children Series

## Life and Lessons of Jesus    Vol. 1

# Jesus' Early Years

Copyright © 1991 by Tracy Leffingwell Harrast.
Published by Cook Communications Ministries.

Printed in the United States of America.

All puzzles and Bible activities are based on the NIV.

Scripture taken from the Holy Bible, New International Version,
Copyright ©1973, 1978, 1984 International Bible Society.
Used by permission of Zondervan Publishing House.

Cover Illustration by Gary Locke

Cover Design by Todd Mock and Mike Riester

Interior Illustrations by Anne Kennedy

Interior Design by Tabb Associates, Mike Riester, and Cheryl Morton

ISBN-10: 0-7814-3847-0
ISBN-13: 978-0-7814-3847-6

101841

# Life and Lessons of Jesus Vol. 1—Jesus' Early Years

# CONTENTS

## Jesus Is Born

# Jesus Grows Up

# Jesus Prepares to Serve

# Jesus Is Born

# Palestine, Where Jesus Was Born

Write **Bethlehem** beneath the nativity scene because that is the name of the city where Jesus was born. Draw the baby Jesus in the manger.

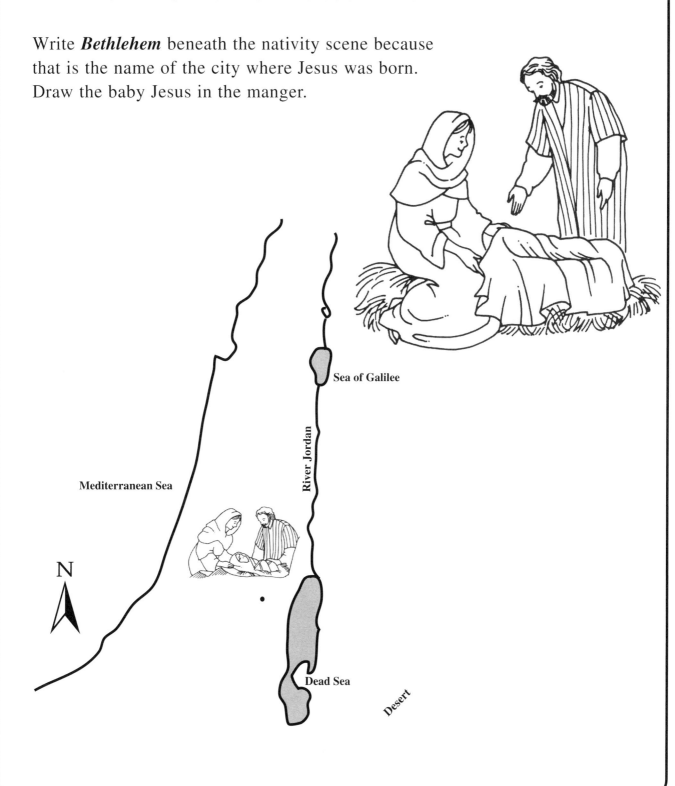

Sea of Galilee

River Jordan

Mediterranean Sea

N

Dead Sea

Desert

# A Christmas Secret

To find the letters that go in the blanks, begin with the letter that follows the dot on the first berry. Write it in the first blank, skip a letter, and put the next letter in the second blank. Continue skipping letters around the berry and writing them in the blanks. When you reach the beginning again, write down the second letter after the dot. Go around the berry again, skipping a letter. When you've circled this berry two times, begin on the next berry.

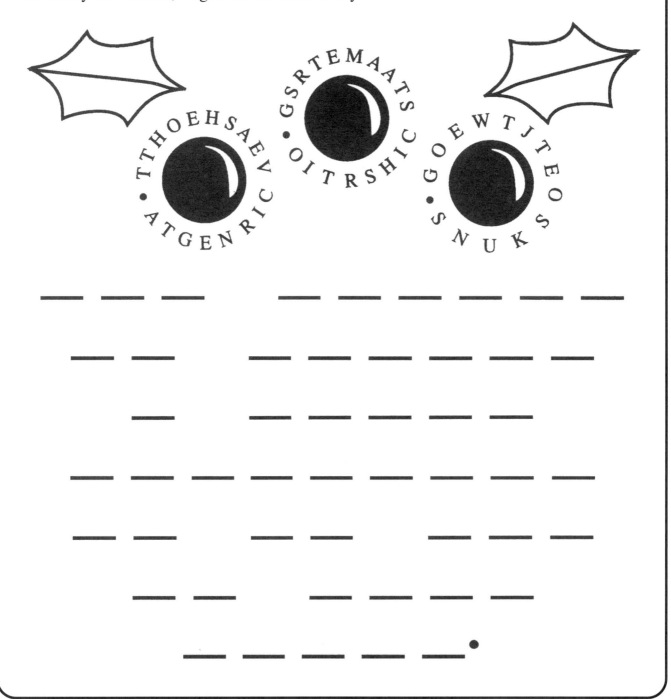

_ _ _ _ _          _ _ _ _ _ _ _ _ _

_ _          _ _ _ _          _ _ _ _ _

_ _          _ _ _

_ _ _ _          _ _ _ _ _ _ _ _ _ _

_ _ _ _          _ _ _

_ _ _ _ _ _ _ _ •

# What Happened When?

Can you put these events from the first Christmas in the order they happened?
Write a number in the box next to each picture. Use the number one for the first event.

# The Meaning Behind Christmas Decorations

Why do people hang wreaths on their doors or put stars on the tops of their evergreen—not oak—trees? Check out some of the meanings behind the Christmas decorations. When you're done reading, color the decorations.

Just as there is no end to a wreath, God's love never ends.

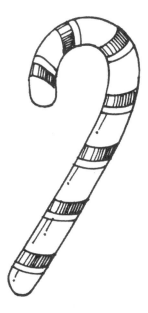

The candy cane is like the shape of a shepherd's staff. A shepherd uses his staff to guide his sheep. The candy cane reminds us that Jesus is our guide as we follow Him.

Evergreen trees stay green all year. They remind us that we can live forever with Jesus.

The lights and stars remind us of the star the wise men followed to find Jesus. In the Bible, Jesus called Himself, "the light of the world."

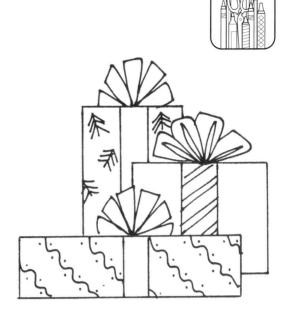

Gifts remind us of the greatest gift ever given—God's gift of His Son, Jesus. Gifts also can remind us of the presents the wise men gave Jesus.

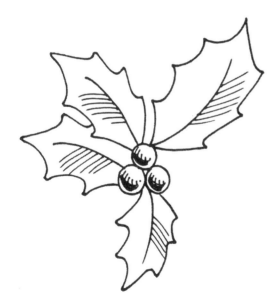

The pointed holly leaves remind us of the crown of thorns Jesus wore as He hung on the cross. The red berries remind us of His blood.

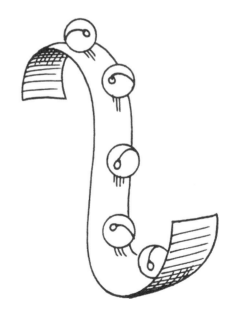

Each sheep in a shepherd's fold wore a bell so the shepherd could tell where it was, if the sheep wandered off. The bells remind us that Jesus knows where we are and wants to save us.

# Make Christmas Wreaths

Wreaths are reminders that God never stops loving you. *Make these wreaths to decorate your home or your classroom.*

## Easy Paper Plate Wreaths

### What You Need

- any size paper plate
- scissors
- paper clip
- duct tape
- popcorn, colored tissue paper, wrapped candies, or green construction paper (depending on which wreath)
- gold spray paint (optional for popcorn wreath) or red ink pad (for handprint wreath)

POPCORN

TISSUE WADS

### What You Do

*1. Draw a circle in the center of any size paper plate.*

*2. Cut out the circle to make a wreath shape.*

*3. Use the tape to attach a paper clip to the back of the wreath to use as a loop for hanging it.*

*4. Glue on popcorn, tissue paper wads, wrapped candies, or handprints cut from green paper onto the paper plate wreath. Let the glue dry.*

*5. If you decorated your wreath with popcorn, you might want to spray paint it gold. If you decorated your wreath with handprints, touch your fingertip on a red ink pad and add fingerprints to the wreath.*

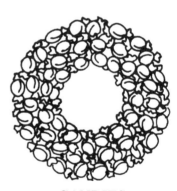

CANDIES

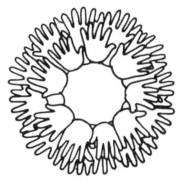

HANDPRINTS

# Cranberry-Popcorn Wreath

## What You Need

- thin floral wire
- frozen cranberries
- popcorn
- red or green ribbon

## What You Do

1. *Bend the floral wire into a circle.*
2. *Push cranberries and popcorn onto the wire until it's nearly full.*
3. *Twist the ends of the wire together; then bend them into a loop for hanging the wreath.*
4. *Tie a ribbon to the loop and make a bow.*
5. *Use an ornament hanger to put the cranberry-popcorn wreath on your Christmas tree. (Note: Be careful not to leave the wreath where it could stain a surface.)*

# Pretzel Wreath

## What You Need

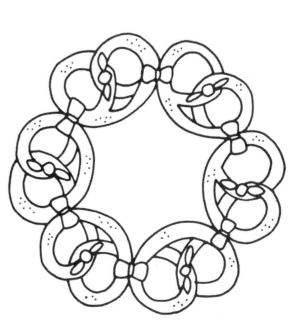

- 6 small pretzel twists (plain or covered with white yogurt)
- six 8-inch pieces of red or green ribbon
- optional: frosting, red and green candied cherries

## What You Do

1. *Arrange pretzels in a circle, as shown.*
2. *Connect the pretzels with ribbons and tie the ribbons into bows.*
3. *If you want to, use frosting to paste on red cherry halves to look like berries and green cherry slices to look like holly leaves.*

# Jesus' Family Tree

Fill in the names of Jesus' ancestors. If you need some help, look up Jesus' family line in Matthew 1:1-17 and Luke 3:23-38.

.. — — — —

(Luke 3:38)
I was the first man.

— — — — —

(Matthew 1:2)
I tricked my father into giving me the family blessing.
Later, I wrestled with an angel.

Æ__ — — — — — — —

(Matthew 1:2)
God changed my name when He promised that I would be
the father of many nations.

Ø — — — — — — — —

(Matthew 1:7)
I became king after my father, David. I was known for my great wisdom.

— — — —

(Matthew 1:16)
I was the mother of Jesus.

± — — — —

(Luke 3:36)
I trusted God to save my family and me from the flood.

— — — — —

(Matthew 1:6)
When I was a young man, I killed a giant named Goliath. I became a
king when I grew up.

# Gabriel Visits Mary

When the angel Gabriel visited Mary, the angel told her some surprising news. Some people call this angel's visit "the Annunciation." *Use your Bible to help you fill in the blanks to find out Gabriel's announcement, and Mary's reply. Also, color the picture.*

Do not be _ _ _ _ _ _ (Luke 1:30). You will give _ _ _ _ _ _ to a _ _ _, and you should name Him _ _ _ _ _ (Luke 1:31). The Holy One to be born will be the Son of _ _ _ (Luke 1:35).

I am the Lord's _ _ _ _ _ _ _ (Luke 1:38).

## Obeying God No Matter What

Mary was willing to be the mother of Jesus even though she knew it might be hard for her. Joseph might have chosen not to marry her since she was expecting a baby. But Mary wanted to do what God wanted. If you want to be like Mary and obey God no matter what happens, color in these letters.

### I WILL DO WHATEVER GOD WANTS ME TO DO

*Draw a star in this box when you've read the story in Luke 1:26-38.*

# An Angel Appears to Joseph in a Dream

Joseph and Mary were betrothed. That meant that they had signed a paper promising to marry each other. When Joseph found out that Mary was expecting a baby, he thought he shouldn't marry her. Sometimes what we think we should do isn't what is really best. That's why we need to ask and trust God— He knows what is best. God sent an angel in a dream to tell Joseph that Mary's baby was God's Son and that Mary and Joseph should get married. He told Joseph to name the child Jesus because He would save His people from their sins.

## Keep a Prayer Journal

Like Joseph learned, listening to God and obeying Him are important things.

God wants to talk to you, too. He may not send angels, but He wants to help you follow Him. When you pray this week, ask God to show you what He wants you to do. On the line beside each day, write these things down; then put a check mark in the box when you've done them.

SUNDAY _____ q

MONDAY _____ q

TUESDAY _____ q

WEDNESDAY _____ q

THURSDAY _____ q

FRIDAY _____ q

☐ *Draw a star in this box when you've read the story in Matthew 1:18-25.*

# Mary Visits Elizabeth

Some of the vowels jumped right out of this story. Can you put them back? Look up Luke 1:39-56, if you need help filling in the missing letters. The vowels are **A, E, I, O, U**.

M_ry w_nt t_ Judea t_ v_s_t h_r c_ _s_n __l_z_b_th. _l_z_b_th _nd h_r h_sb_nd, Zechariah, w_r_ _xp_ct_ng a b_by, wh_ w_ _ld b_ J_hn th_ B_pt_st.

As s_ _n _s __l_z_b_th h_ _rd M_ry's v_ _c_, h_r b_by j_mp_d f_r j_y _ns_d_ h_r. __l_z_b_th c_ll_d M_ry "th_ m_th_r _f my L_rd" _nd s_ _d, "You are bl_ss_d _nd s_ _s y_ _r b_by."

M_ry praised G_d. She said, "My soul glorifies th_ L_rd _nd my sp_r_t rejoices _n G_d my S_v_ _r. From n_w on _ll generations w_ll c_ll m_ bl_ss_d, for th_ Mighty One h_s done gr_ _t th_ngs for m_. H_ly _s H_s name."

## Praise God Like Mary Did

Write a praise poem or sentences about how great God is and why you love Him. Then say your poem or sentences as a prayer to God.

_____

_____

_____

_____

_____

*Draw a star in this box when you've read the story in Luke 1:39-56.*

# Extra Special News: Jesus Is Born

To read this extra special story about the first Christmas, cross out the extra letter in each word. You can find the story in Luke 2:1-7 in your Bible.

*Extra Special News...*
*Jesus is Born!*

Taxxes ared mfoney speople pray top theird scountry's pleaders. Backt zin Bibble timmes, peoople thad top play toheir staxes min sperson. Tox dor thist, Marry band Josteph thraveled frovm theird homeltown Nazarethx pin Galileex tom Bethlehemb tin Judeaw.

Marey wass tabout tox havel ay barby, buth thre qinn whhere theyy sttopped wast fully. Sor Marfy shad tow giver birdth cin as stablet. Shem wrapperd Jesust gin stripst lof clothz calleds swaddlingx clothest sand laird thim pin at mangerw (at brox fort vanimal frood).

☐ *Draw a star in this box when you've read the story in Luke 2:1-7.*

# Make a Nativity Scene from Dough

## What You Need

- 12 slices of white bread (without crusts)
- 1 teaspoon dishwashing liquid
- white glue
- water
- paintbrush
- paint
- newspaper
- lacquer
- piece of felt

## What You Do

1. *Crumble the bread into tiny pieces in a bowl. Then add 4 tablespoons of glue and one teaspoon of dishwashing liquid. Stir with a spoon until the dough is mixed well.*

2. *Then knead (or shape) the dough with your hands until the dough isn't sticky. If it's too dry, add a few drops of glue. If it's too sticky, add a little more bread.*

3. *Spread newspaper to cover the table. Form the dough into a simple nativity scene. To help prevent cracking, paint the figures with a mixture of 8 tablespoons glue and 8 tablespoons water. Let the figures dry overnight and then paint. When the paint is dry, spray the figures with lacquer.*

4. *When everything is dry, arrange the nativity scene on a piece of felt.*

# Christmas Card Finger Puppets

*Make these puppets from old Christmas cards. When you're not playing with them, they can serve as a nativity scene because the loops keep them standing!*

## What You Need

- old Christmas cards with nativity scenes on them
- parent's permission
- scissors
- cellophane tape

## What You Do

1. *Cut off the backs from one or two cards, and then cut them into ten strips about 1/2 inch wide.*

2. *Bend each strip into a loop so it fits around one of your fingers. Tape each loop together, tearing off any extra part of the strips.*

3. *Cut out nativity scene figures from the fronts of the cards, and tape a loop to each figure.*

4. *Tell the Christmas story, using your finger puppets.*

# Angels Visit Shepherds

God chose to announce the good news of His Son's birth to the shepherds. To read this special announcement, fix the spacing in this story from Luke 2:8-20. The first sentence has been done for you.

The|night|Jesus|was|born, shepherds|were|watching|their|flocks. Suddenlyawholegroupofangelscametothemandsaid, "Don'tbeafraid.Webringgoodnewsthatwillgivegreatjoy toallpeople.Todayyour Savior,ChristtheLord,wasborn inBethlehem.You'llknowyou'vefoundHimwhenyoufinda babywrappedinswaddlingclothesandlyinginamanger."

Theangelsbeganpraising Godandsaying"GlorytoGodin thehighest.Peaceandgoodwilltoall."Whentheangels returnedtoheaven,theshepherdshurriedandfoundMary andJosephandthebaby.

Thentheshepherdstoldeveryoneabouttheangelsand thenewbornbaby.Maryrememberedallthese thingsandthoughtaboutthem.

*Draw a star in this box when you've read the story in Luke 2:8-20.*

# Make a Tootsie Pop Shepherd

In Bible times, shepherds didn't have a lot of power or popularity. Yet God chose to tell them the wonderful news of His Son's birth. Later, when Jesus was an adult, He called Himself the Good Shepherd who takes care of His sheep. Candy canes are the shape of shepherds' staffs to remind us that Jesus wants everyone to follow Him.

## What You Need

- Tootsie Pop
- peach or tan, white, and blue facial tissues
- peach or tan pipe cleaner
- two small rubber bands
- piece of twine
- ballpoint pen
- tape
- candy cane
- scissors

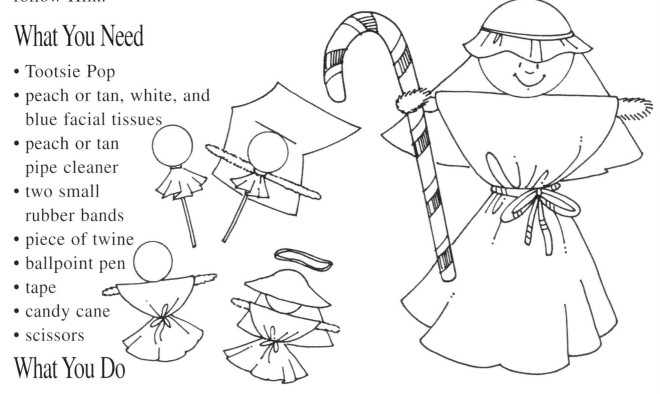

## What You Do

1. *Cover the Tootsie Pop with a peach or tan tissue. Wrap a rubber band under the lollipop to make the shepherd's head.*

2. *Twist the pipe cleaner several times around the lollipop's stick near the top.*

3. *Fold the blue tissue lengthwise. Cut or tear a small slit as shown.*

4. *Put the blue tissue over the shepherd's head. If necessary, tape the slit closed underneath. Tie the twine as a belt.*

5. *Cut the white tissue as shown. Put it on the shepherd's head and secure it with a rubber band.*

6. *Draw a face and any other details you want to add.*

7. *Twist one of the shepherd's hands around the candy cane. Hang the shepherd on your Christmas tree.*

# God's Messengers: Angels

At different times, angels visited Mary, Joseph, and the shepherds with messages about Christ's birth. The messages the angels brought each of them are hidden in the puzzle. Find the first word of each message in the puzzle, and the rest of the message is connected to that word. You can move up or down, backward or forward to find the message. Write the messages in the blanks.

To Mary: YOU __ __ __ __   __ __ __ __   __ __ __ __ __   __ __   __ __ __ __

__ __ __   __ __   __ __ __ __.

To Joseph: DO __ __ __   __ __   __ __ __ __ __ __ __   __ __   __ __ __ __ __

__ __ __ __.

To shepherds: YOUR __ __ __ __ __ __ __   __ __ __   __ __ __ __   __ __ __ __ __ __.

```
D D O K A F O R D I A R F A E S T U
L S M D P N E Q T A D C B E B W F V
J Q V U B M I J O G (D O) N O T B Q R
R L B R G L D K M K G H F Y Z C H E
V J N B C H T S A U J W E M H D A Y
N (Y O U) R O P L R I X F L X G N I A
B S T W N J C D R V O N H I J D M D
B T N I B A I H Y M A R Y A E Z A O
T A R L C J G V U S G P R K L O P T
F E R L G I V E T Q X E W S B O R N
U T M F E D K B X I F O J A D B Y C
O O P N T M L I A B H G I W R Z U D
B Q R S (Y O U R) S A V I O R T S V O
P N V L W R Z T Y C F E K Y Q X W G
K G A M N O D H T O T H E S O N O F
```

# Paper-Plate Angel with Handprint Wings

## What You Need

- paper plate
- glitter
- glue
- markers
- yellow construction paper
- tape

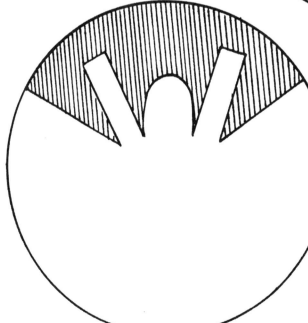

**PATTERN**
(Not actual size)

## What You Do

1. Draw a pattern like the one below on the bottom of a paper plate and cut it out.

2. Draw a face on the plate.

3. Tape together the angel's robe.

4. Tape the angel's hands together.

5. To make the wings, trace your hands on the yellow construction paper. Cut out the handprints. Outline them with glue and sprinkle with glitter. Let dry.

6. Tape the wings to the back of the angel.

# Wise Men Worship Jesus

Wise men from the East traveled to Bethlehem to worship Jesus. Read this story from east to west to find out about their journey.  The story is from Matthew 2:1-12.

and find to wanted they because star a followed East the from men Wise
could they where asked they ,Jerusalem reached they When .Jesus worship
.Jews the of king born was who one the find
they when angry were Jerusalem in people many and Herod ruler evil The
and together leaders religious Jewish the called Herod King .this about heard
told They .born be would Jesus said had Scriptures the where know to demanded
Then .star the seen had they time what men wise the asked Herod  .Bethlehem him
When .child the for look and "Go ,said and Bethlehem to them sent he
,Actually ".too ,Him worship and come can I so me tell ,Him found have you
.Jesus kill to wanted Herod
them of ahead went following been had they star the ,left men wise the When
the saw they When .was child young the where over stood and came it until
saw and house the entered they When .happy very were men wise the ,star
Then .Jesus worshiped and down fell they ,Mary ,mother His with child young the
.myrrh and ,frankincense ,gold of gifts Jesus gave and treasures their up opened they
went they So .Herod to return to not dream a in them warned God Afterward
.way different a home back

*Draw a star in this box when you've read the story in Matthew 2:1-12.*

# Make a Wise Man Candy Crown

## What You Need

- 20" x 6" strip of poster board or other cardboard
- scissors
- stapler
- wrapped candies
- cellophane tape or glue

## What You Do

1. *Cut notches or other designs along one side of the strip. Wrap the strip around your head to form a crown. When the ends are overlapped the right amount to fit your head, staple the ends together.*

2. *Glue, tape, or staple candies onto the crown.*

3. *Wear your crown and pretend you're a wise man following a star, visiting Herod, bringing gifts, and worshiping Jesus. Sing the Christmas carol, "We Three Kings."*

4. *When you're finished playing, eat the crown's jewels.*

# Magi Crossword

*Solve this crossword puzzle about the wise men, or Magi, who came from the East to worship Jesus, the king of the Jews. If you need help, look in Matthew 2:1-12.*

## ACROSS

1. Where Jesus was born.
2. By the time the wise men found Jesus, He was in a _____.
3. The wise men told this wicked king about Jesus' birth.
4. The wise men were warned in a _____ not to return to Herod.
6. The wise men felt this emotion when they saw the star stand still.
7. The wise men were from this area.
8. A gift the wise men brought to Jesus.

## DOWN

1. The Jewish leaders told Herod that a prophet had said Jesus would be a _____ of His people.
2. One of the gifts the wise men gave Jesus.
3. This guided the wise men to Jesus.
4. A precious metal the wise men gave Jesus.
5. Jesus was with His _____ when the wise men arrived.
6. The wise men were looking for Him.

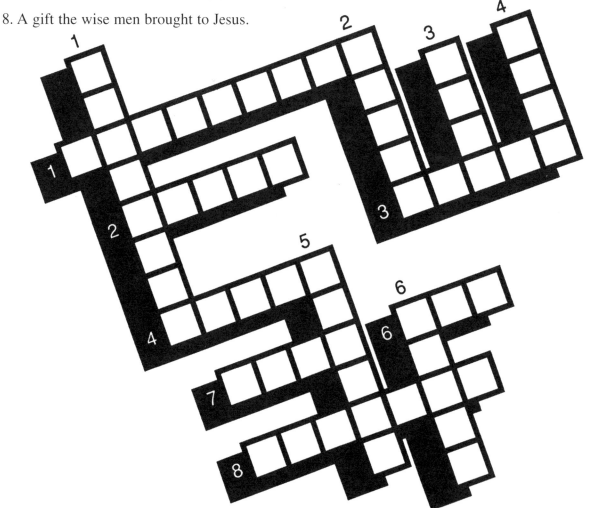

# Starry Treats for Christmas

Enjoy a special "star"-filled breakfast on Christmas morning. Then later on in the day, enjoy another starry treat. Here are two recipes for you to follow. Be sure to get an adult to help you when you work in the kitchen.

## BREAKFAST STARS

### What You Need

- two or three slices of bread for each serving
- one egg for every three slices of bread
- star-shaped cookie cutter
- butter or margarine
- one cup powdered sugar
- milk
- cinnamon
- paper lunch bag

### What You Do

1. Crack open eggs in a large bowl. Add a tablespoon of milk and a dash of cinnamon. Beat eggs rapidly with a fork.
2. Cut as many stars as possible from the slices of bread.
3. Dip each star in the egg mixture.
4. Ask a grown-up to help you fry both sides of the stars in butter or margarine until they are golden brown.
5. Pour powdered sugar into the paper sack. Drop a fried star into the sack, close the sack, and shake it. Take out the star and repeat with other stars until all of them are coated with powdered sugar. Serve them right away.

## FUN LEMON STARS

### What You Need

- two small packages of lemon gelatin (3 oz. size)
- one cup boiling water
- grown-up help

### What You Do

1. Pour gelatin into a bowl.
2. Ask a grown-up to help you boil a cup of water and pour it into the bowl.
3. Stir the mixture until the gelatin is completely dissolved.
4. Pour it into an 8-inch square baking dish.
5. Chill the gelatin until it is firm.
6. When it's firm, cut out shapes with a star-shaped cookie cutter. Use a spatula to take out the stars from the pan.

# Star Luminarias

In Mexico, a Christmas tradition is to set out luminarias on Christmas Eve. It's said that the luminarias light the way for Mary, Joseph, and the baby. *Color this picture and prepare to light a path to the door of your home with some luminarias.*

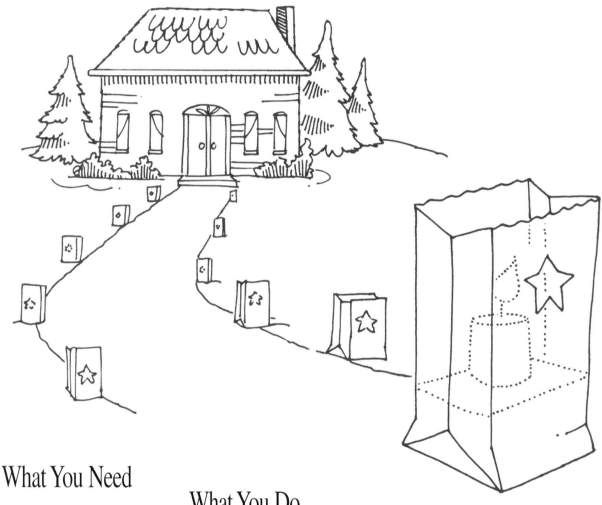

## What You Need

- 10 brown paper lunch sacks
- pencil
- scissors
- enough sand to put 4 inches in each bag (sold in gardening and hardware stores)
- ten votive candles

## What You Do

1. *Fold down the top of each sack about one inch.*
2. *Draw a star on each sack and cut out the stars.*
3. *Pour about four inches of sand into each sack.*
4. *Stick a candle into the sand in each sack.*
5. *Evenly space the bags along your sidewalk.*
6. *Ask a grown-up to help you light the candles. The flame on each candle will go out when the candle burns down to the sand.*

# A Wise Idea

*Cross out every Christmas word in this puzzle that is found in the border of this page. When you are finished, you will find a wise idea for you to follow!*

GIFTS STOCKINGS THE SANTA WISE
FRUITCAKE MEN ORNAMENTS
MUST NATIVITY TREE HAVE
WREATH BELLS BEEN HOLLY
CLOSE  EVERGREEN TO GOD TO
CARDS KNOW THEY GINGERBREAD
WERE SUPPOSED CANDY CANES TO
PACKAGES FOLLOW MANGER THE
STAR NUTCRACKER TO REINDEER
FIND JESUS. ICICLES STAY MERRY
MERRY CLOSE TO RIBBON GOD
GIFTWRAP SO BOWS HE CAN
BERRY GUIDE YOU.

# Give Gifts to Jesus

In Matthew 25:40, Jesus says that when we do kind things for other people, we are doing those things for Him, too. *On the gifts, write the names of people you know and some kind things you can do for them. When you give away these "gifts," remember that you're also giving them to Jesus.*

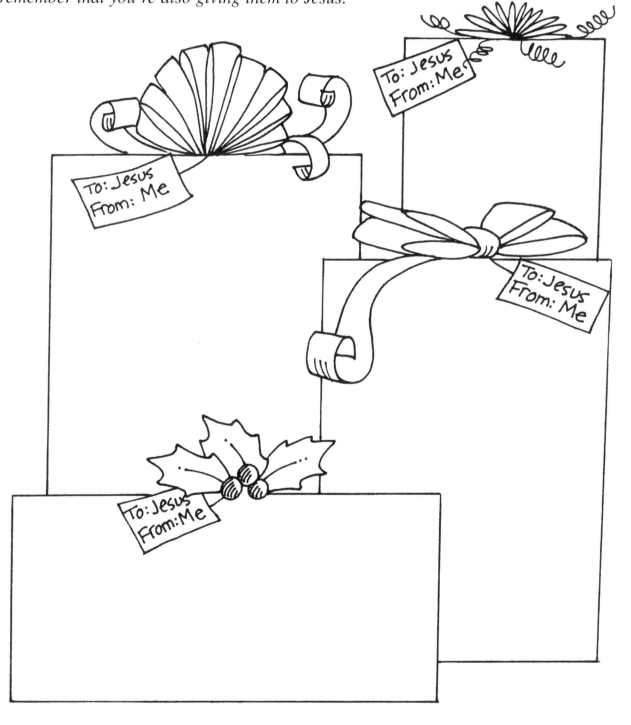

# The Best Gift Ever Given

God loved all of us so much that He sent His Son, Jesus, to live on earth. (Read about this in John 3:16). Jesus came to die for the wrong things we've done. This made it possible for us to live forever with God.

People give you gifts because they love you, not because you have earned them. To receive a gift that someone offers you, you have to accept it. That's what God wants you to do with His gift of eternal life.

If you want to accept God's gift, you can pray a prayer similar to this one.

Dear God,

Thank You for sending Your Son, Jesus. I believe He died for my sins so I can live forever with You. I accept Him as my Savior. Please forgive me of the wrong things I've done and make me the way You want me to be. I will trust Jesus as my Savior and will follow Him all of my life. I love You.

In Jesus' name.

Amen.

*If you have accepted the gift of eternal life, sign your name and the date here. Then tell the person who gave you this book or page.*

_____  _____
NAME                                              DATE

# Christmas Gifts to Make

*Thank God for His gift to you as you give gifts.*

## Homemade Bibs for the Baby

### What You Need

- new, inexpensive, plain washcloths
- permanent markers
- two pinching-style clothespins
- 6-inch piece of ribbon or yarn

### What You Do

1. *Decorate the washcloths and clothespins with markers.*
2. *Tie each end of the ribbon or yarn to a clothespin.*
3. *Attach the clothespins to a washcloth to make a bib.*

## Refrigerator Magnets for Mom or Grandma

### What You Need

- tracing paper or tissue paper
- pencil
- scraps of felt
- scissors
- glue
- magnets (from craft stores)

### What You Do

1. *Trace the designs onto tracing paper or tissue paper.*
2. *Cut out the tracing paper or tissue paper designs and use them as patterns to cut the designs from felt.*
3. *Glue the felt pieces together as shown.*
4. *Glue a small magnet to the back of each design and let dry.*

## Lunch Bag Puppets for Young Brothers and Sisters

### What You Need

- package of inexpensive paper lunch sacks
- markers
- scraps of colored paper
- glue stick

### What You Do

*Decorate a month's supply of lunch bags as puppets, so your brother or sister has a fun toy after finishing his or her lunch each day.*

# A Personalized Clipboard for Teen Brothers or Sisters

## What You Need

- clipboard
- paint, pens
- friends and family of the teenager

## What You Do

*Ask family and friends of the teenager to autograph the clipboard with paint pens.*

# Peanut Butter Swirl Candy for Dad

## What You Need

- 1 cup powdered sugar
- 6 teaspoons of milk
- peanut butter

## What You Do

1. Pour powdered sugar into a large bowl.

2. Stir after adding each teaspoon of milk. You may not need all of the milk.

3. Stop adding milk when you have a dough you can handle easily. If it's too sticky, add a little more powdered sugar. If too dry, add milk one teaspoon at a time.

4. Sprinkle powdered sugar on a clean counter top or waxed paper.

5. Roll out the dough 1/4 inch thick using a rolling pin or drinking glass dipped in powdered sugar.

6. Spread a thick layer of peanut butter over the dough.

7. Roll the dough up like a jelly roll.

8. Chill it until stiff.

9. Slice it into candies with a plastic knife and put the candies into a jar you have decorated.

# A Crayon Porcupine for a Brother, Sister, or Friend

## What You Need

- piece of thick styrofoam
- scrap paper
- pencil
- scissors
- permanent markers
- crayons
- colored ribbon
- grown-up help

## What You Do

1. Draw a porcupine with pencil on the scrap paper.
2. Cut out the porcupine and ask the grown-up to use it for a pattern to cut out the Styrofoam.
3. Decorate the Styrofoam porcupine with permanent markers.
4. Poke a hole with the pencil for each of the crayons that the porcupine will be holding. Insert the crayons.
5. Tie a ribbon around the porcupine's neck.

# Christmas Stick Puppets and Stage

Watching Christmas programs is fun, and it's even more fun to perform one yourself. Here's a chance to put together your own Christmas program for your family and friends.

Photocopy, color, and cut out the puppets from page 37. Next, tape the puppets to craft sticks or spoon handles so you can move them around.

You might want to perform the Christmas stories on pages 16-19, 22, and 26 for your family and friends.

## Puppet Stage Backdrops

*Now that you have your puppets, make a stage for your performance. With your brothers and sisters or your friends, practice your puppet show. Choose a date to perform your Christmas program for your family or other friends.*

## What You Need

• three small boxes (shoe box size)
• crayons, markers • scissors

## What You Do

1. *To make the stage and scenery, draw and color backdrop scenes on the inside bottoms of three small boxes. One scene is the inside of a house, one scene is outdoors, and one scene is the stable where Jesus was born. See patterns on page 38.*

2. *Make a slit across the bottom of each box. (Cut the slit near one of the long sides of the box. Plan to set up the stage boxes on the edge of a table.) Stick the puppets through the slit and move them across the "stage" that way.*

3. *Use the inside of a house for Mary and Elizabeth, Joseph's dream, and the visit of the wise men. Use the outdoor scene for Mary and Gabriel, the trip to Bethlehem, and the shepherds. Use the stable scene for when Jesus was born.*

Gabriel

Mary

Elizabeth

Baby Jesus

Innkeeper

Joseph

Shepherds

Angels

Child Jesus

Wise Men

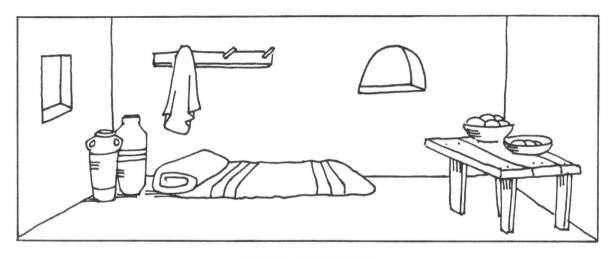

INSIDE OF HOUSE

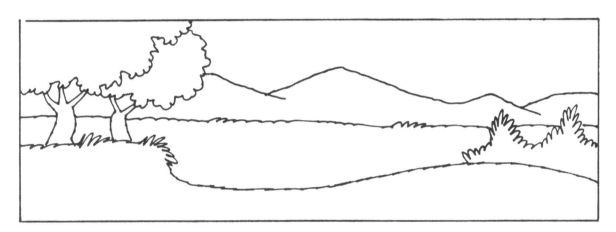

OUTDOOR SCENE

STABLE

# Plan a Class or Family Christmas Program

Make this Christmas special. Plan a Christmas program in which you and your class or family worship the Lord together. Use this sample program for ideas. As you plan your own program, include traditions that have special meaning for your class or family. You can copy the sample program and fill in your own ideas.

## Sample Program

1. *Open with prayer, thanking God for the gift of His Son, Jesus.*
2. *Sing "Silent Night."*
3. *Display a picture of Jesus and take turns telling why you are glad He was born.*
4. *Use homemade puppets to perform the story of the first Christmas. A class or family member may read the story from Luke 2:1-19. Or give each person one or two nativity pieces to place around the nativity stable as a class or family member reads Luke 2:1-19.*
5. *Sing "Away in a Manger."*
6. *Point out Christmas decorations on the tree or around the room, and talk about their meanings.*
7. *Sing "Angels We Have Heard on High."*
8. *Close in prayer, thanking God for Jesus' birth.*

Our _____ (year) Christmas Program

Prayer by _____ (name of class or family member)

Song, "_____"

A Christ-centered activity:_____

A presentation of the first Christmas from Luke 2:1-19

Song, "_____"

A Christ-centered activity:_____

Song, "_____"

Prayer by _____ (name of class or family member)

# Throw a Birthday Party for Jesus

*Celebrate the true meaning of Christmas with your family, friends, or class by throwing a birthday party for Jesus.*

# Games and Activities

- Play "Pin the Tail on Mary's Donkey."
- Play musical chairs, using Christmas carols as the music.
- Decorate star-shaped cookies.
- Make birthday cards for Jesus.
- Sing "Happy Birthday" to Jesus just before cutting the cake.
- My idea: _____
- My idea: _____

# Party Decorations

- Hang red and green crepe paper streamers and balloons from the ceiling.

- Set up several nativity scenes around the room.

- Make posters that say, "We love Jesus." Only use two candy canes to make a heart shape to use instead of the word "love."

- My idea: _____

- My idea: _____

# Refreshments

- Have a cake decorated with white, red, and green icing that says "Happy Birthday, Jesus!"

- Serve raspberry and lime sherbet or vanilla ice cream with red and green sugar sprinkles on top.

- My idea:_____

- My idea:_____

# Advent Activity Calendar

## What You Do
*Remove pages 42 and 43/44 from this book. Cut along the dashed lines on page 44. Carefully put a thin line of glue along the dotted lines below (pg. 42). Place page 44 over page 42 and tape edges.*

Tie 24 wrapped candies together with ribbon. Number the candies 1 through 24. Eat one each day until Christmas.

Decorate a tree for the birds with popcorn strings and bread cut into Christmas shapes with cookie cutters.

Read Luke 1:26-38. Think about how you would have felt if you were Mary.

Plan a birthday party for Jesus.

Decorate your lunch bag with Christmas symbols. At lunchtime, tell your friends the meanings of the symbols.

Dip string in glue and wrap a balloon. Let it dry in a warm spot. Pop the balloon and hang your ornament.

Read Matthew 1:18-25. Think about how you would have felt if you were Joseph.

Stick a chenille wire through some jingle bells. Bend it into a circle. Shake it as you sing a Christmas carol.

Glue craft sticks together to make a star. Paint or cover it with glitter. Hang the star on your tree.

Cut a Christmas shape out of a sponge. Paint one side of the shape and use it to stamp some homemade cards.

With a good friend, sing your favorite Christmas carols. Afterward, drink some hot chocolate.

Read Luke 2:1-7. How would you have felt if you were there when Jesus was born?

Write the names of carols on strips of paper. Take turns acting out the songs without using any words.

Make a jigsaw puzzle out of last year's Christmas cards (with parent's permission).

Read Luke 2:8-20. How would you have felt if you were a shepherd that night?

Cut one end off a potato. Poke holes and insert sprigs from an evergreen tree. Decorate your little Christmas tree.

Use some of last year's Christmas cards as gift tags (with parent's permission).

Make a lunch, using only red and green foods (with parent's permission).

Cut Christmas shapes out of felt and glue onto plain ornaments (with parent's permission).

Read Matthew 2:1-12. Does the Bible say there were exactly three wise men?

Make thank-you notes from scraps of gift wrap.

Have open-face sandwiches for lunch. Top the sandwiches with cheese cut into Christmas shapes.

Thank God for the gift of His Son, Jesus.

Perform a puppet show about the first Christmas for your family.

The word Advent means "coming." Advent season begins four Sundays before Christmas. During Advent, we look forward to the coming of Jesus and His birth. As you wait for the coming of Christmas Day, open one window each day and do the activity you find under that window.

# I Did It!

| COMPLETED | DATE | COMPLETED | DATE |
|---|---|---|---|
| ☐ Palestine, Where Jesus Was Born | _____ | ☐ Tootsie Pop Shepherd | _____ |
| ☐ A Christmas Secret | _____ | ☐ God's Messengers: Angels | _____ |
| ☐ What Happened When? | _____ | ☐ Wise Men Worship Jesus | _____ |
| ☐ The Meaning Behind Christmas Decorations | _____ | ☐ Make a Candy Crown | _____ |
| ☐ Make Christmas Wreaths | _____ | ☐ Magi Crossword | _____ |
| ☐ Jesus' Family Tree | _____ | ☐ Starry Treats for Christmas | _____ |
| ☐ Gabriel Visits Mary | _____ | ☐ Star Luminarias | _____ |
| ☐ Obeying God No Matter What | _____ | ☐ A Wise Idea | _____ |
| ☐ Angel Appears to Joseph | _____ | ☐ Give Gifts to Jesus | _____ |
| ☐ Keep a Prayer Journal | _____ | ☐ The Best Gift Ever Given | _____ |
| ☐ Mary Visits Elizabeth | _____ | ☐ Christmas Gifts to Make | _____ |
| ☐ Extra Special News: Jesus Is Born | _____ | ☐ Christmas Stick Puppets and Stage | _____ |
| ☐ Make a Nativity Scene from Dough | _____ | ☐ Plan a Class or Family Christmas Program | _____ |
| ☐ Christmas Card Finger Puppets | _____ | ☐ A Birthday Party for Jesus | _____ |
| ☐ Angels Visit Shepherds | _____ | ☐ Advent Activity Calendar | |

# Jesus Grows Up

# Palestine, Where Jesus Grew Up

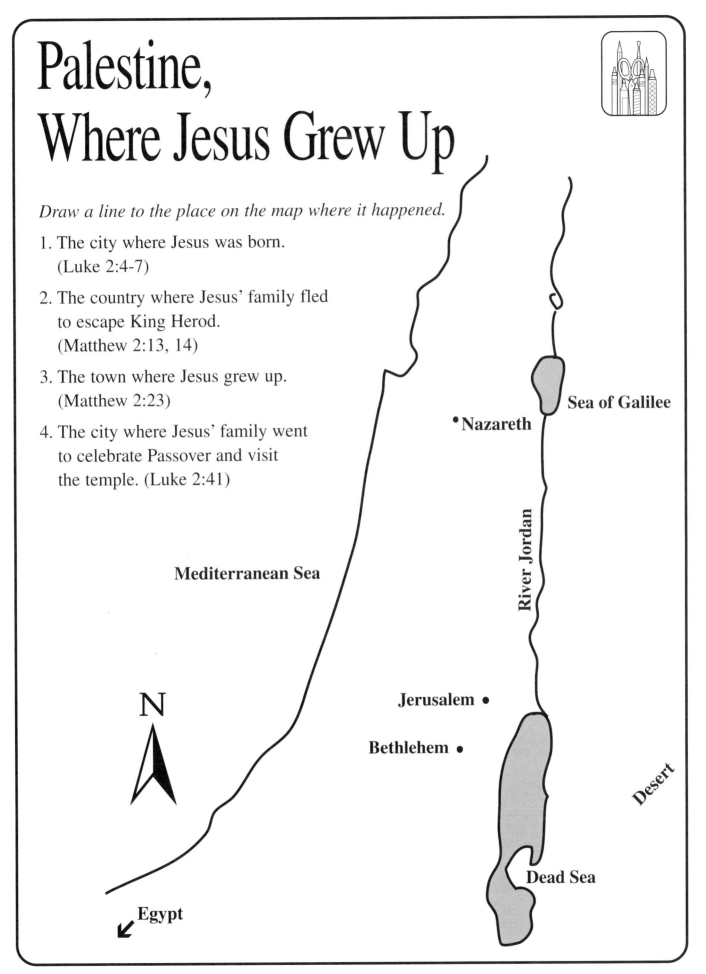

*Draw a line to the place on the map where it happened.*

1. The city where Jesus was born.
   (Luke 2:4-7)

2. The country where Jesus' family fled
   to escape King Herod.
   (Matthew 2:13, 14)

3. The town where Jesus grew up.
   (Matthew 2:23)

4. The city where Jesus' family went
   to celebrate Passover and visit
   the temple. (Luke 2:41)

Sea of Galilee

•Nazareth

River Jordan

Mediterranean Sea

**N**

Jerusalem •

Bethlehem •

Desert

Dead Sea

Egypt

# What's That?

*How well do you know the story of Jesus' birth? Read about it in Luke 2:1-7 in the King James Bible. Then, draw a line from each word to what it means. Then draw a line from the meaning to the picture it matches.*

**Swaddling**

1. A place where animal feed was kept. In Bible times, it was usually carved in a wall.

**Manger**

2. A place where animals were kept. In those days, some were caves.

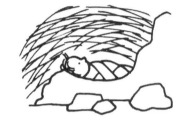

**Stable**

3. Clothes for wrapping a baby.

**Inn**

4. Money that was paid to the leaders of the country.

**Tax**

5. A place for people to stay when they traveled.

*Draw a star in this box when you've read the story in Luke 2:1-7.*

# When Was Jesus Born?

HEROD DIED ⟶

8 7 6 5 4 3 2 1 • 1(A.D.) 2 3 4 5 6 7 8

THE CREATION ◁ B.C.(BEFORE CHRIST)     A.D. (ANNO DOMINI) ▷ NOW

Almost 600 years after Jesus was born, the calendar was changed so that years would be counted by whether they were before or after the birth of Jesus. The years before Jesus was born were labeled B.C. (Before Christ). The years were counted backward from the time Christ was born. For example, the year 5 B.C. came before the year 4 B.C. The years after Jesus was born were called A.D. (Anno Domini, which means "in the year of our Lord").

*Use the facts below to figure out when Jesus might have been born.*

FACT: Matthew 2:1 says Jesus was born while Herod was king.

FACT: Herod died in the year 4 B.C.

FACT: Matthew 2:16 shows that Jesus may have been at least two years old when Herod died.

1. What is definitely the latest date that Jesus could have been born? (Hint: the year Herod died) _____

2. What year is likely the earliest year Jesus could have been born? (Hint: two years before Herod died) _____

3. How many years has it probably been since Jesus was born? (Hint: add your answer from question #2 to the current year) _____

If you made a birthday cake for Jesus this year, how many candles should it probably have? (Your answer from question #3.) *Write that number on the cake.*

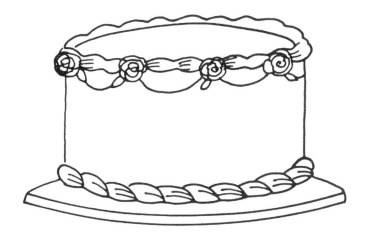

# What a Little Bird Tells Us about Joseph and Mary

*Read these words and pictures to discover an interesting fact about Jesus' parents, Mary and Joseph.*

W+ 🐑 👶👶  were  b + 🌽 - c,  🍐 + ents

h + 😠 - m  2  t + 🎂 - c  A 🐑 and A

🐦 2 the 🏛 .  If  th + A  were

temple

p + 🚪 - d,  th + A could  b + 💍 2 🐦 .

It is  1 + 🚲 - b + ly  t + 🎩 👤 and 👤 were

Joseph          Mary

p + 🚪 - d  🐝 + cause  th + A  brought  A

2nd 🐦 and 🪢  A 🐑 .

Draw a star in this box when you've read the story in Luke 2:21-24.

# Find Out What Simeon Said

When you play "Simon Says," you do only what Simon says, not what he doesn't say. In this game, you'll do what Simeon says, not what Simeon doesn't say. Simeon saw Jesus at the temple and said this about Him.

Simeon says, "Change every A to O
　　　　and every O to A."
　　　　Change every B to Z
　　　　and every Z to B.
　　　　Change every Y to R
　　　　and every R to Y.
Simeon says, "Change every I to E
　　　　and every E to I."
Simeon says, "Change every S to M
　　　　and every M to S."

Thi Haly Mperet hod tald o son nosid Mesian thot hi wauld nat dei

_____

untel hi mow thi pirman wha wauld movi thi warld. Whin hi mow

_____

thi boby Jimum, Mesian moed, "Naw, E con dei en pioci." Hi kniw

_____

Jimum wom thi ane wha wauld movi thi warld. O wason nosid

_____

Onno kniw et, taa. Da yau knaw et?

_____

☐ _Draw a star in this box when you've read the story in Luke 2:25-35._

# Jesus Escapes to Egypt

Someone was trying to kill the young Jesus! Read about His escape to Egypt. Use the code to help you translate the story from "hieroglyphics" (Egyptian picture writing) into English.

**Code:**

m = Angel      ÷ = Egypt      ⬥ = Dream      🍁 = king

⚹ = Jesus      ⇁ = Joseph      ☼ = Mary      🦌 = throne

An m _____ appeared to ⇁ _____ in a ⬥ _____ and told him to take ☼ _____ and ⚹ _____ to ÷ _____ and to stay there until the m _____ told him to bring them back. The m _____ said the cruel 🍁 _____ would try to kill ⚹ _____. ⇁ _____ obeyed.

Herod was probably afraid that ⚹ _____ would grow up and take his place on the 🦌 _____. After 🍁 _____ Herod died, ⇁ _____, ☼ _____, and ⚹ _____ moved to Nazareth in Galilee.

☐ *Draw a star in this box when you've read the story in Matthew 2:13-23.*

# Make a Pyramid

Joseph obeyed God and took his family to Egypt. God wanted to protect Jesus. God's commands are always what will help us. Like Joseph, we can trust God's plans for us and obey Him. This week, after you pray and read your Bible, think of things God wants you to do and write them on the outside of your pyramid. When you've obeyed God, color that particular side of the pyramid.

## What You Need

- typing paper
- pencil
- scissors
- tape

## What You Do

1. *Trace the pyramid pattern on this page onto the piece of typing paper.*
2. *In your own words, write the things you can do to obey and follow God this week.*
3. *Cut out your pyramid. Fold it along the dotted lines so plans to obey God are on the outside of the pyramid. Tuck in the tab, and tape it.*

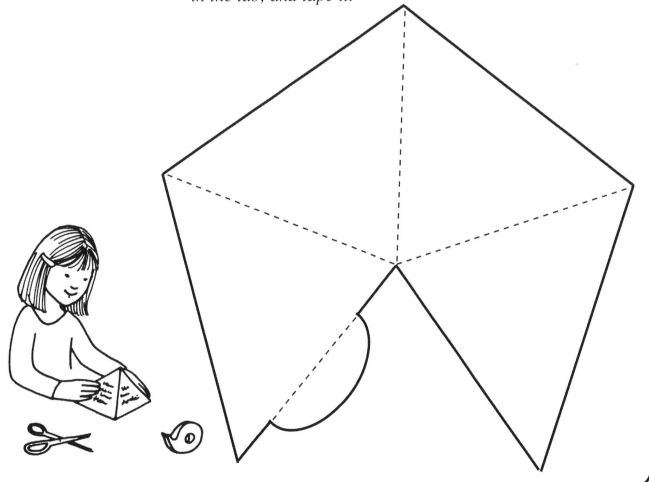

# Clothes in Jesus' Day

Have you ever wondered what kind of clothes people in Bible times wore? They obviously didn't wear jeans and T-shirts. Jesus probably wore clothes like these when He was a boy.

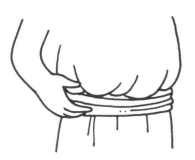

The TUNIC was a short- or long-sleeved piece of clothing that came down to the knees or ankles. Poor people wore tunics made of goat's or camel's hair. This was rough material. Wealthy people wore tunics made of wool or linen, colored with expensive dyes.

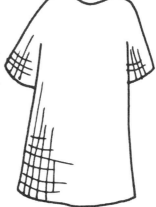

Instead of carrying a wallet, people pulled up their tunics to make a pouch above their belts where they carried valuables. This was called the BOSOM.

The belt was sometimes called the GIRDLE. When people needed to run or move freely, they pulled their tunics up through their girdles to leave their legs uncovered. This was called "girding up your loins."

Some people, usually the poor, had CLOAKS that were more like a blanket than a coat. People wore them mostly in cool weather, and sometimes they covered their heads with them. At night they could wrap themselves in their cloaks to keep warm. People who had more money wore cloaks that were more like simple coats.

Underwear was similar to shorts and was made of linen or leather. It was called a WAISTCLOTH.

SANDALS were made of leather and had a flat sole. Two straps ran across the top of the foot and between the toes.

# What Jesus Probably Wore

*Write the name of each article of clothing in the blank next to it.*

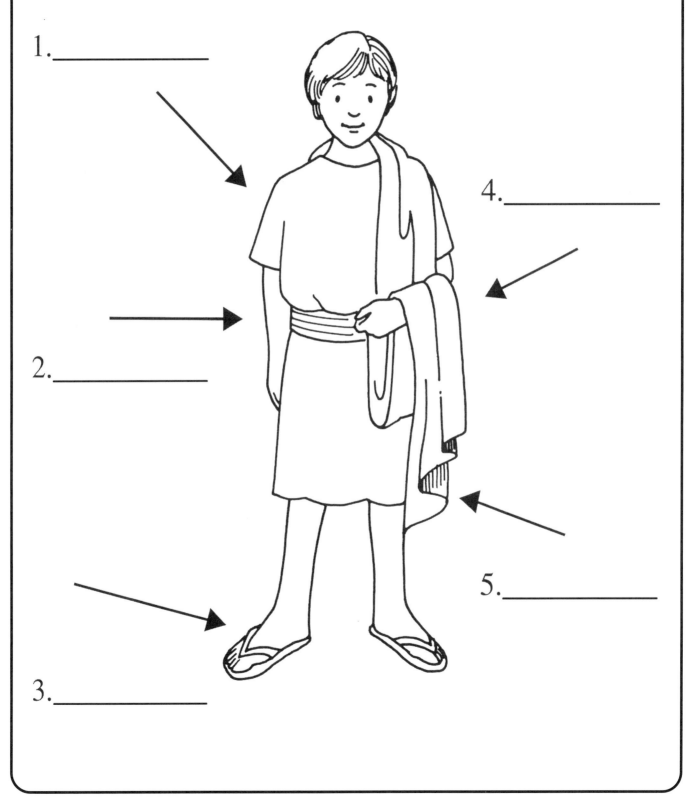

1._____

2._____

3._____

4._____

5._____

# The Languages Jesus Spoke

## ARAMAIC    GREEK    HEBREW

Jesus probably spoke at least three languages. He likely spoke Aramaic at home and with His friends. He spoke Hebrew when studying the Scriptures in the synagogue (Jewish church) and at school. He probably spoke Greek as well.

You may know and use some Hebrew words. Two Hebrew words are often used in worship. One means "praise the Lord." You might use this word in a worship song or psalm. Do you know what it is? *Unscramble these letters to discover the Hebrew word:* JLLAHAUELH 1. _ _ _ _ _ _ _ _ _ _

Another word means "so let it be." You usually say this word at the end of your prayers. Do you know what it is? *Unscramble these letters to discover the Hebrew word:* MAEN 2. _ _ _ _

## The Greek Alphabet

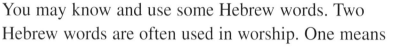

Here are the letters of the Greek alphabet. Try pronouncing the letters.

| A | alpha | H | eta | N | nu | T | tau |
|---|---|---|---|---|---|---|---|
| B | beta | Θ | theta | Ξ | xi | Υ | upsilon |
| Γ | gamma | I | iota | O | omicron | Φ | phi |
| Δ | delta | K | kappa | Π | pi | X | chi |
| E | epsilon | Λ | lambda | P | rho | Ψ | psi |
| Z | zeta | M | mu | Σ | sigma | Ω | omega |

# The Fish of Faith

After Jesus died, Christians were treated badly for their belief in Him. Many were put in prison or killed. Early Christians began using a symbol to let other Christians know secretly that they, too, believed in Jesus. The symbol looked like this:

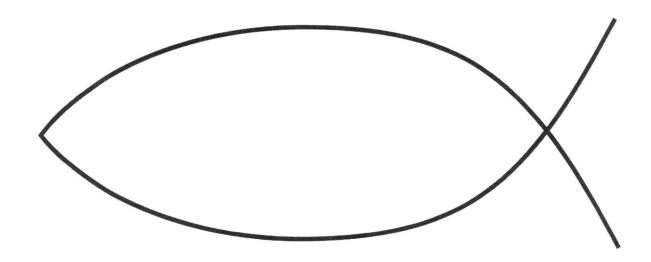

The Greek letters iota, chi, theta, upsilon, and sigma spell the word fish in Greek and were written inside the fish symbol. *Write those letters in the fish symbol above using the Greek alphabet on page 58. Each letter stood for a Greek word. The words were Jesus Christ, God's Son, Savior.*

*Use the Greek letters on page 58 to write out the words below. Notice that the first letter of each word is found in the fish symbol above.*

**Jesus** (iota eta sigma omicron upsilon sigma ) __ __ __ __ __ __

**Christ** (chi rho iota sigma tau omicron sigma) __ __ __ __ __ __ __

**God's** (theta epsilon omicron upsilon) __ __ __ __

**Son** (upsilon iota omicron sigma) __ __ __ __

**Savior** (sigma omega tau eta rho) __ __ __ __ __

# Money in Bible Times

The most common coin in Jesus' day was a denarius. This was a day's pay for a farm worker as well as a soldier. We don't know how much a denarius was worth.

Pretend that a worker today would earn $20.00 a day. That means that a denarius today would be worth $20.00. *Compare each coin with the denarius to figure out how much it might be worth today. Write the amount on each coin.*

**DENARIUS**
Day's pay
for an average worker

**TALENT**
Worth 6,000 denarii*
(6,000 x $20)

**AUREUS**
Worth 25 denarii*
(25 x $20)

**STATER**
Worth 3 denarii*
(3 x $20.)

**DIDRACHMON**
Worth 1¹/₂ denarii*
(1¹/₂ x $20)

**DRACHMA**
Equal to 1 denarius

**ASSARION**
About 20 made 1 denarius
($20 ÷ 20)

**KODRANTES**
About 80 made 1 denarius
($20 ÷ 80)

**LEPTON**
About 160 made 1 denarius
($20 ÷ 160)

*Denarii is the plural form of denarius.

# The Family of God

Jesus' family doesn't just include the people shown as puppets in this book. Everyone who accepts and follows Jesus is born again into the family of God. Complete this short puzzle to find out about God's family.

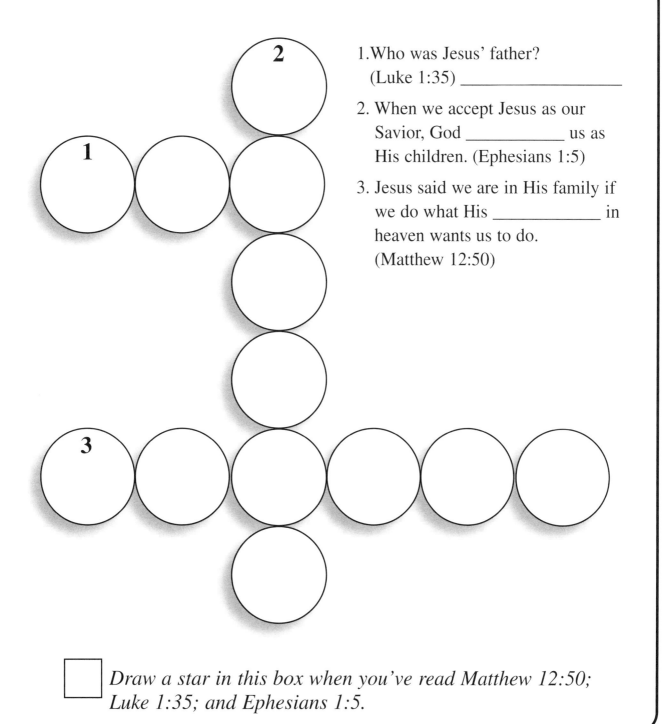

1. Who was Jesus' father? (Luke 1:35) _____

2. When we accept Jesus as our Savior, God _____ us as His children. (Ephesians 1:5)

3. Jesus said we are in His family if we do what His _____ in heaven wants us to do. (Matthew 12:50)

*Draw a star in this box when you've read Matthew 12:50; Luke 1:35; and Ephesians 1:5.*

# Becoming Part of God's Family

Have you asked Jesus to save you from your sins and trusted Him as the only way you can live with God in heaven forever? If you have, then you're a member of God's family along with everyone else who trusts and follows Jesus! If you have questions about becoming a part of God's family, ask the person who gave you this page or book to explain more about accepting Jesus as your Lord and Savior.

## The Family of God

*These people have a good reason to be happy—they belong to God's family. However, there's one person who's missing and that's you. Finish drawing yourself to complete this picture of God's family.*

# House Matchups

*Match things from your house with things from Jesus' house.*

### Your House

### Jesus' House

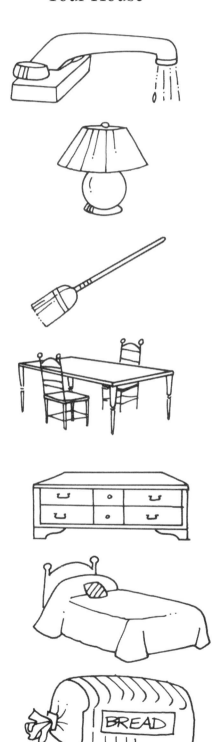

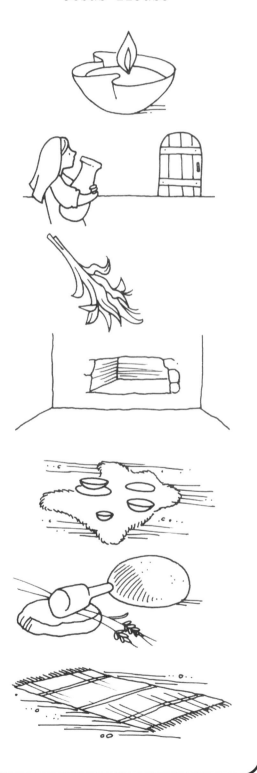

# Make a Bible-Times House

*Use the puppets from page 62 to act out what you think life may have been like in Jesus' home in Nazareth. Remember that Hebrews 4:15 tells us that Jesus never sinned.*

The roof was probably made of branches with clay on top of them. It would have been very leaky. After a rain, people had to roll roofs out with a big roller to make them flat again. People spent a lot of time on the roof. Roofs had short walls or railings that kept people from falling off.

## What You Need

• shoe box  • pudding box  • brown paper  • scissors  • tape  • markers  • glue
• potting soil  • colored cutouts from pages 67 and 68

## What You Do

1. *Cover the outside of the shoe box and the inside walls with brown paper and tape the paper in place. The houses in Jesus' day were usually made of clay bricks, so draw bricks with markers.*
2. *The houses in Jesus' day usually had dirt floors, so coat the bottom with glue and sprinkle potting soil on it.*
3. *Cut out holes for windows. Jesus' windows would not have had any glass in them.*
4. *Tape the pudding box shut and cover it with brown paper. Cut a piece of paper and fold it to look like stairs. Glue the box to the floor of the house and glue the "stairs" to the box and to the floor. This makes a platform where the family worked and slept. They usually kept animals inside the house on the lower floor.*
5. *The walls behind the platform had places carved out of them that stored sleeping mats and cooking utensils. The floor of the platform had a hole carved out of it for storing corn and other food; this was covered with a clay lid. The walls had troughs carved out of them that held animals' food. Cut these out from page 68 and glue them onto the wall behind the platform.*
6. *Cut out the other items from pages 67 and 68 and stand them inside the house or glue them onto the walls.*

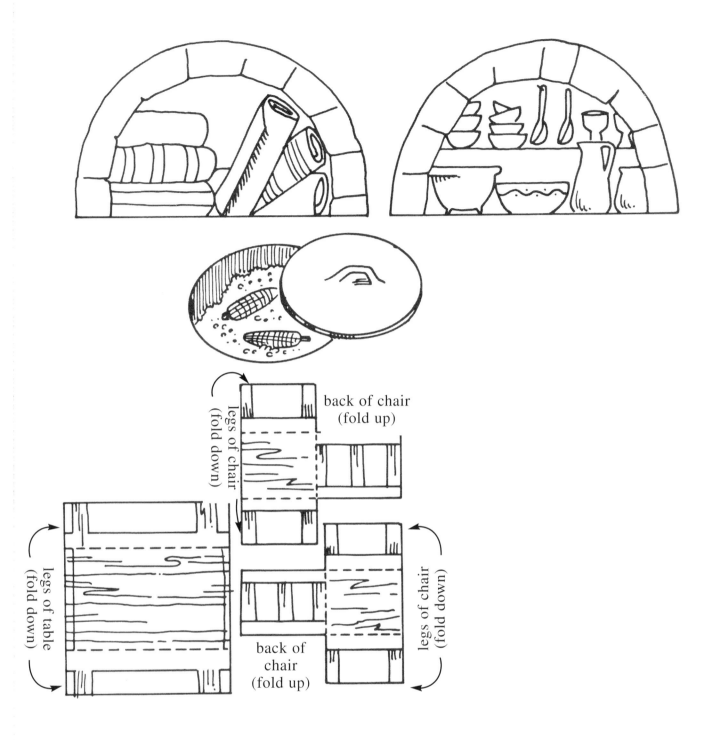

back of chair
(fold up)

legs of chair
(fold down)

legs of chair
(fold down)

legs of table
(fold down)

back of
chair
(fold up)

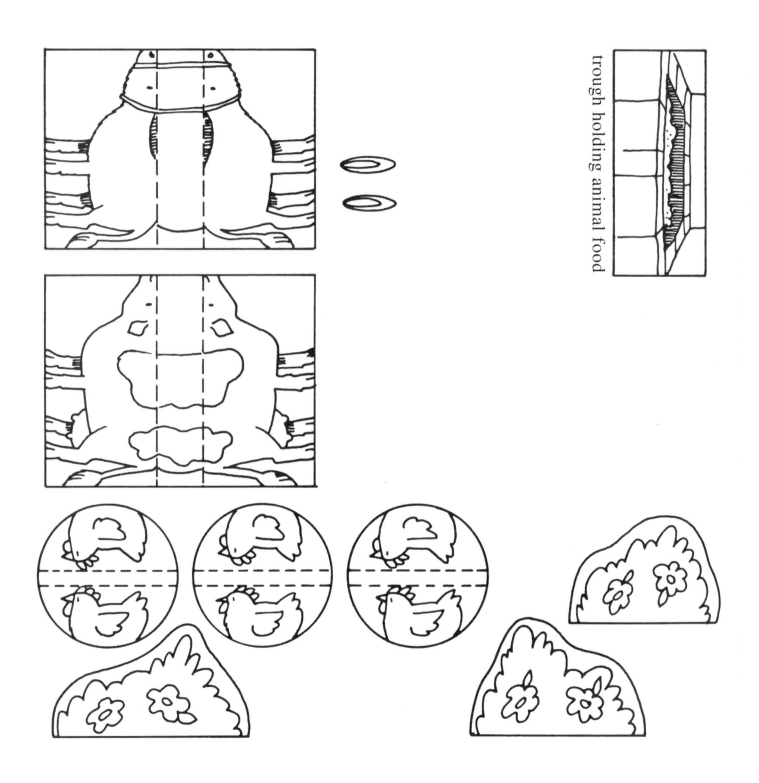

trough holding animal food

# Woodworking with Joseph

Joseph was a carpenter. In Bible times, fathers usually trained their sons to do the same job they did, so Jesus probably learned woodworking. They may have made yokes (wooden bars that keep two animals joined while they are working together), wheels, troughs to hold animal food, and simple furniture.

Some people think Joseph may have died while Jesus was a teenager because Joseph isn't mentioned in the Bible after Jesus was twelve years old. If so, Jesus may have had to help earn a living for Mary and the rest of the family.

*If you can, visit someone who does woodworking. As you watch him or her work, think about Jesus and Joseph. Think about how their tools would have been similar and different (remember that they didn't have electricity). Ask for some sawdust to take home for sawdust clay.*

## Sawdust Clay

### What You Need

- 1 cup sawdust
- 1 cup flour
- 3/4 cup water

### What You Do

1. *Mix sawdust and flour together in a medium-size bowl.*
2. *Slowly add water, stirring until a dough forms. (You may not need all of the water.) If the clay is too dry, add a little more water. If it is too wet, add equal amounts of sawdust and flour.*
3. *After you have shaped the clay into an object, let it dry two or three days. Then you can sand it and paint it.*

# Play Bible-Times Games

In Jesus' day, Jewish children often played a game called "The Gap."

## What You Need

• 12 pebbles

## What You Do

*Gently toss 12 pebbles upward. Flip your hand over and try to catch as many pebbles as you can on the back of your hand. Whoever catches the most pebbles wins.*

## 'Jacob and Rachel'

Jewish children played this game that was based on an Old Testament story in which Jacob was tricked into marrying the wrong girl! He ended up with Leah when he wanted to marry Rachel.

## What You Need

• 1 boy and at least 2 girls

## What You Do

1. *The boy stands in the middle of a circle of girls. The girls are holding out an arm to him.*
2. *He closes his eyes and the girls walk around him until he grabs a hand.*
3. *Without opening his eyes, he tries to guess whose hand he is holding.*

If you are playing in a group that has more than one boy, boys should take turns being Jacob or there should be more than one circle of kids playing the game at the same time.

# Holidays Jesus Celebrated

The word *holiday* comes from the words *holy* and *day*. In Old Testament times God told His people to celebrate special holy days each year. All Jewish males age twelve and older had to travel to Jerusalem for three feasts every year. They were 1) Feast of the Passover and Unleavened Bread, 2) the Feast of Weeks or Pentecost, and 3) the Feast of Tabernacles. What Jewish holidays are marked on your calendar?

## Passover (held in March or April)

To find out about Passover, first read the story and pass over every word that has a cross above it. When you reach the end, read the story a second time, reading only the words with the crosses above them. *Color the door frame red like the blood of the Lamb if you have accepted Jesus as your Savior.*

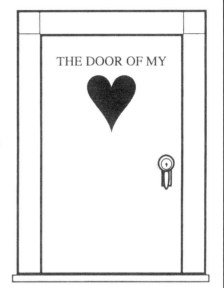

THE DOOR OF MY ♥

The anyone. Passover Jesus was called when Himself Jewish the people Passover remembered lamb. the His night blood God delivers delivered us them from from sin slavery and in we Egypt. can The trust people Christ killed to a forgive lamb us. and He put died its on blood the on cross the for doorposts. us The so angel we passed can over live these forever homes in and heaven didn't someday. kill

# Holidays Jesus Celebrated

## Feast of Unleavened Bread (held immediately after Passover)

*Cross the letters that spell "leaven" out of each word to find out about this feast.*

Wleahevenn Gleaovd'sen pleeavopenle (Ilseavraeenlites)
lweeavreen flreeeadven flreaovmen slleaavveenry leiavenn
leEagvyepnt, lteahveeyn leleafvetn tloeaoven qleuiavckelny
lteoaven pluetaven leavenleaven (wlehaavten mleaavkeesn
lebavreenad rleaivseen leaanvend bleeavcoenme
lleaigvhent) lineaven leatvheen leabvreenad ledavoughen.
leaAvfteenr tlehaavetn, tlheeayven hleealvend letahveen
lFeaeavsetn loeafven Unleavenleavened Brleaeavden
leaeavcehn lyeaeavren.

Dleaurvening lteavheen fleaeavenst tlheeaveny leavenonly
leaavteen flleaatven, unleavenleavened blreaeadven
fleavenor aleaven weeleavenk leaanvend tlheaanvkeend
Gloeavend fleavenor tleaakveinng thleeavmen leaouvetn
olfeaven slealavvenery.

Most supermarkets sell unleavened bread you can buy to taste. It's called matzo.

# Holidays Jesus Celebrated

## Feast of Weeks or Pentecost (held 50 days after Passover)

This was a celebration of joy and it was a time when people thanked God for the blessings of a good wheat harvest. *Write or draw pictures of some of your blessings and thank God for them.*

ETH LYOH
TISPRI

What did the early Christians receive on the Day of Pentecost after Jesus went to heaven? (See Acts 2:4.)

# Holidays Jesus Celebrated

## Feast of Tabernacles (held in September or October)

The word tabernacle means *tent*. The Feast of Tabernacles was celebrated to remember that God's people lived in temporary shelters when God brought them out of Egypt. The feast was held when the fruit from the orchards had been harvested. People visiting Jerusalem, and even the people who lived in the city, camped in huts and tents like ones the children of Israel stayed in after they left Egypt.

### *Praise God in a tent like the Jews did during the Feast of Tabernacles*

*Make a tent from chairs and a blanket. Take a picnic of fruit into the tent and thank God for blessing you with food to eat and for taking care of you like He took care of His people in the wilderness. Color the picture on this page.*

# Taste Foods Jesus Ate

When your parents are making up a grocery list, ask them to add a few of these foods that Jesus ate. Think about Jesus as you try some of the foods He ate.

barley bread

grape juice

salt

olive oil

cumin spice

pomegranates

fish

onions

figs

almonds

honey

raisins

grapes

dates

pistachio nuts

olives

# Make Grape Juice

Grapes were one of the main crops in the land where Jesus lived. Sometimes people used a press to crush grapes and drain the juice to make wine. Or they actually stepped on them with their bare feet! Try your hand—er, that is, your feet—at making some grape juice. Ask an adult to help you.

## What You Need

- 1 pound of red seedless grapes • newspaper • paper towels
- gallon-size sealable plastic bag • cardboard box
- large, sterile gauze bandages or cheesecloth

## What You Do

1. *Spread newspapers on the floor to protect it.*
2. *Wash the grapes and pull them off the stems. Then drop the grapes into the plastic bag. Squeeze the air out of the bag and seal it.*
3. *Lay the bag of grapes in a large cardboard box on top of the newspaper.*
4. *Take off your shoes and socks, and very carefully walk on the bag until the juice is mashed out of the grapes.*
5. *Hold a clean gauze bandage or piece of cheesecloth over a glass and carefully pour juice from the bag into the glass. When the glass is full, throw away the gauze and what it has strained out of the grape juice.*
6. *Enjoy your grape juice! Share it with your class or family.*

# School in Jesus' Day

Jewish places of worship were called synagogues (try to say that word ten times fast!) Each had a school attached to it. A Jewish boy began attending school at age five or six. Only boys went to school. There, the boys learned to read and study the Scriptures. Every child memorized the Shema, a group of Scriptures from the book of Deuteronomy.

*For each blank, find the letter that has the same number and put it in that blank. Then memorize this verse (Deuteronomy 6:4, 5) that all Jewish boys, including Jesus, memorized.*

A=17  B=25  C=19  D=12  E=49  F=71  G=3  H=15  I=4  J=1
K=39  L=20  M=7  N=14  O=2  P=5  Q=8  R=21  S=52  T=9
U=34  V=22  W=16  X=42  Y=26  Z=56

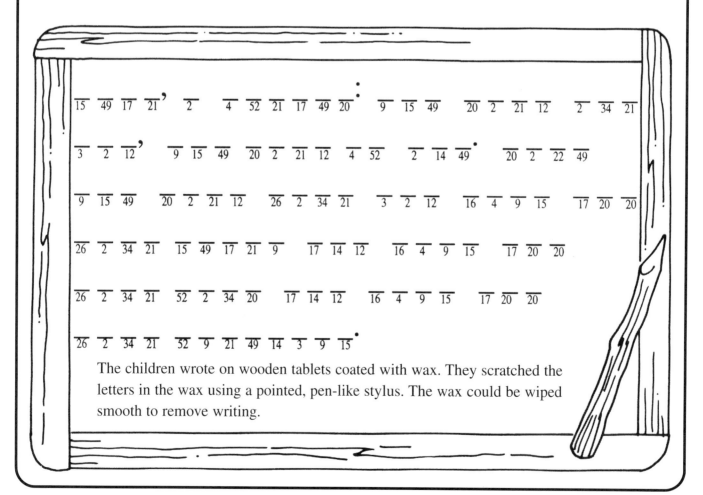

——  ——  ——  ——  ,  ——    ——  ——  ——  ——  ——  ——    ——  ——  ——    ——  ——  ——  ——    ——  ——  ——
15  49  17  21      2     4  52  21  17  49  20     9  15  49    20   2  21  12     2  34  21

——  ——  ——  ,  ——  ——  ——  ——  ——  ——  ——  ——    ——  ——  ——    ——  ——  ——  ——
 3   2  12      9  15  49  20   2  21  12   4  52     2  14  49    20   2  22  49

——  ——  ——    ——  ——  ——  ——    ——  ——  ——  ——    ——  ——  ——    ——  ——  ——  ——    ——  ——  ——
 9  15  49    20   2  21  12    26   2  34  21     3   2  12    16   4   9  15    17  20  20

——  ——  ——  ——    ——  ——  ——  ——  ——    ——  ——  ——    ——  ——  ——  ——    ——  ——  ——
26   2  34  21    15  49  17  21   9    17  14  12    16   4   9  15    17  20  20

——  ——  ——  ——    ——  ——  ——  ——    ——  ——  ——    ——  ——  ——  ——    ——  ——  ——
26   2  34  21    52   2  34  20    17  14  12    16   4   9  15    17  20  20

——  ——  ——  ——    ——  ——  ——  ——  ——  ——  ——  ——  ——  ——
26   2  34  21    52   9  21  49  14   3   9  15

The children wrote on wooden tablets coated with wax. They scratched the letters in the wax using a pointed, pen-like stylus. The wax could be wiped smooth to remove writing.

_nd_rst_nd_ng  _nd  _nsw_rs.
  30      31          55

M_ry  s_ _d,  "S_n,  why  h_ve  Y_ _  tr_ _t_d  _s
              32

l_k_  th_s?  Y_ _r  f_th_r  _nd  _  h_ve  b_ _n
33                          34    35

s_ _rch_ng  f_r  Y_ _  _nd  h_ve  b_ _n  v_ry  _ps_t."
    36    37                      38      39

J_s_s  s_ _d,  "Why  w_r_  y_ _  s_ _rch_ng  f_r
            40                41 42    43

M_?  D_dn't  y_ _  w_nt  M_  t_  b_  d_ _ng  My
45

F_th_r's  w_rk?"
      46

_t  th_  t_m_,  M_ry  _nd  J_s_ph  d_dn't  _nd_rst_nd
          47                                        48

th_t  J_s_s  w_s  t_lk_ng  _b_ _t  G_d  th_  F_th_r.
                                            49

B_t  M_ry  r_m_mb_r_d  wh_t  J_s_s  h_d  s_ _d.
  51    50          54      52    53

*Fill in the blanks to find something this story teaches.*

‾1‾ ‾2‾ ‾3‾ ‾4‾ ‾5‾  ‾6‾ ‾7‾ ‾8‾  ‾9‾ ‾10‾ ‾11‾  ‾12‾ ‾13‾ ‾14‾ ‾15‾

‾16‾ ‾17‾ ‾18‾ ‾19‾ ‾20‾  ‾21‾ ‾22‾  ‾23‾ ‾24‾ ‾25‾  ‾26‾ ‾27‾ ‾28‾ ‾29‾ ‾30‾

‾31‾ ‾32‾  ‾33‾ ‾34‾ ‾35‾ ‾36‾ ‾37‾  ‾38‾ ‾39‾ ‾40‾  ‾41‾ ‾42‾ ‾43‾ ‾44‾ ‾45‾

‾46‾ ‾47‾ ‾48‾  ‾49‾ ‾50‾ ‾51‾ ‾52‾ ‾53‾ ‾54‾ ,  ‾55‾ ‾56‾ ‾57‾ .

# Growing Like Jesus

Luke 2:40 says Jesus "grew and became strong; he was filled with wisdom, and the grace of God was upon him." Make a growth chart to see how you're growing. Each time you measure your height, ask yourself, "Have I grown to be a little more like Jesus?"

## A Growth Chart to Make

### What You Need

- 6 feet of 1-inch wide bias tape
- measuring tape
- permanent markers
- scissors
- stapler
- paper hole punch
- adhesive tape

I Want to Grow Like Jesus Did

Growth Chart Holder

### What You Do

1. *Ask a grown-up to help you iron out the creases in the bias tape.*
2. *Using a measuring tape and markers, draw small lines one inch apart along an edge of the bias tape.*
3. *Start at what will be the bottom of the growth chart and count up to the twelfth mark. Write a large numeral 1 beside this mark. Count 12 marks from here and write a numeral 2. Count 12 marks from the numeral 2 and write a numeral 3. Count 12 marks from this mark and write a numeral 4, etc.*
4. *Cut out the growth chart holder and fold it in half. Color it and punch out the hole.*
5. *Place the top of the bias tape inside the holder and staple it.*
6. *Hang the growth chart so the bottom of it barely touches the floor. Tape the bottom of the chart to the wall.*
7. *Measure your height by standing next to the chart.*

 *Draw a star in this box when you've read Luke 2:40.*

# Jesus Obeyed His Parents

Luke 2:51 says that Jesus was obedient to His parents. Are you?

*Underneath each of these faces, write something that your mom or dad told you to do today or yesterday. If you obeyed without complaining the first time your parent asked, draw a smile on the face. If you complained, had to be asked more than once, or disobeyed, draw a frown. Three smiles in a row make you a winner. Frowns don't win no matter how many are in a row.*

☐ *Draw a star in this box when you've read Luke 2:51.*

# Grow Four Ways Jesus Grew

Luke 2:52 says "Jesus grew in wisdom and stature, and in favor with God and men." You can grow in these ways, too. *Look at the four ways Jesus grew and try to complete the goals for each way. As you complete each goal, color the goal's picture.*

## 1.) In Wisdom (His mind grew)

For a whole day, think before you speak.

Before going to sleep, think about what you did during the day. What did you do well? Were there some things you could have done better? Ask God to help you with these things

Read the Bible each day for a week.

## 2.) In Stature (His body grew)

Cut out junk food for a day, and eat only healthy snacks.

Get to bed on time every day for a week.

Get some exercise every day for a week.

# 3.) In Favor with God (His spirit grew)

Accept Jesus as your Savior. (Trust Him to make you able to go to heaven.)

Pray every morning and evening for a week.

Learn a new song, and then sing it as a praise to God.

# 4.) In Favor with People (His personality grew)

Make a new friend.

Say only nice things for a day.

For a day, put yourself in everyone else's shoes. Each time you talk to someone, try to understand why he acts and feels the way he does.

# What Would Jesus Do?

Jesus was once young like you. He understands what you're going through, because He became a person and lived on earth. When you're in difficult situations, ask Jesus to help you do what He would do in your situation. *For each of these situations, circle the answer that would help you become more like Jesus. When you're done, put the letters of the answers you circled in the blanks at the bottom of page 85 to find out how Jesus wants you to treat others.*

**1. Someone unpopular wants to eat lunch with you.**

**B.** Be nice, but eat as fast as you can.
**L.** Try to become friends and maybe introduce her to others.
**J.** Tell her you already promised to eat with someone else (even though you didn't).

**2. One of your friends is thinking of taking drugs.**

**A.** Say, "That may be okay for you, but I won't do it."
**O.** Ask an adult to explain why taking drugs is bad. Then explain it to your friend.
**K.** Don't say anything.

**3. A friend says she's ashamed of something she did wrong.**

**D.** Act shocked and say, "I would never do something like that!"
**E.** Say you won't play with someone like that.
**V.** Tell her God loves us and will forgive us when we do wrong things if we ask Him and put faith in Jesus.

**4. Your brother has been yelling and slamming doors.**

**B.** Tell your parents they ought to punish him.
**E.** Try to figure out what's bothering him and fix him a snack while you're fixing one for yourself.
**H.** Tell him to stop because he's putting you in a bad mood.

**5. Someone copies your test and tells the teacher you copied hers.**

**M.** Tell everyone she's a cheater and to watch out for her.

**O.** Tell her you don't like her, and figure out how to get revenge.

**T.** Tell her how that made you feel and then forgive her.

**6. A friend says she hopes she can do enough good things to get to heaven.**

**H.** Tell her that we could never do enough good things to get to heaven. Encourage her to come to accept Jesus as Savior and follow Him.

**N.** Say, "You're such a nice person I'm sure you'll go there."

**D.** Don't say anything.

**7. One of the kids at church doesn't come very often. How do you treat him?**

**J.** Be glad you're a better person and don't say anything to him.

**R.** Tease him so he'll feel bad about not coming and will come more often.

**E.** Help him figure out why he doesn't come more and encourage him.

**8. There's a new kid at school. What do you do?**

**K.** Wait to see who makes friends with him before becoming his friend.

**M.** Introduce yourself and try to make him feel comfortable.

**D.** You already have enough friends, so don't say anything.

**When you want to treat people as Jesus would, all you have to remember is to . . .**

— — — — —  — — — —.

# I Did It!

| COMPLETED | DATE | COMPLETED | DATE |
|---|---|---|---|
| ☐ Palestine, Where Jesus Grew Up | _____ | ☐ House Matchups | _____ |
| ☐ What's That? | _____ | ☐ Make a Bible-Times House | _____ |
| ☐ When Was Jesus Born? | _____ | ☐ Woodworking with Joseph | _____ |
| ☐ What a Little Bird Tells Us about Joseph and Mary | _____ | ☐ Play Bible-Times Games | _____ |
| ☐ Find Out What Simeon Said | _____ | ☐ Holidays Jesus Celebrated | _____ |
| ☐ Jesus Escapes to Egypt | _____ | ☐ Taste Foods Jesus Ate | _____ |
| ☐ Make a Pyramid | _____ | ☐ School in Jesus' Day | _____ |
| ☐ What Jesus Probably Wore | _____ | ☐ Where Jesus Worshiped | _____ |
| ☐ The Languages Jesus Spoke | _____ | ☐ Somebody and Something's Missing | _____ |
| ☐ The Fish of Faith | _____ | ☐ Growing Like Jesus | _____ |
| ☐ Money in Bible Times | _____ | ☐ Jesus Obeyed His Parents | _____ |
| ☐ Jesus and His Family | _____ | ☐ Grow Four Ways Jesus Grew | _____ |
| ☐ The Family of God | _____ | ☐ What Would Jesus Do? | _____ |
| ☐ Becoming a Part of God's Family | _____ | | |

# Jesus Prepares to Serve

# Palestine, Where Jesus Served

Jesus was born in Bethlehem. Draw a manger on that city.

Jesus learned and taught in the temple at Jerusalem. Draw a temple there.

Jesus was baptized near Bethabara in the Jordan River. Draw a dove there.

Philip, Peter, and Andrew were from Bethsaida. Circle it three times.

Peter, Andrew, James, and John were fishermen on the Sea of Galilee. Draw a fish in the sea.

Matthew (whose name was Levi before Jesus changed it) was a tax collector in Capernaum. Draw a dollar sign on that city.

Nathanael (also called Bartholomew) whom Jesus saw under a tree was from Cana. Jesus said he would see angels going into and out of heaven. Draw an angel on Cana.

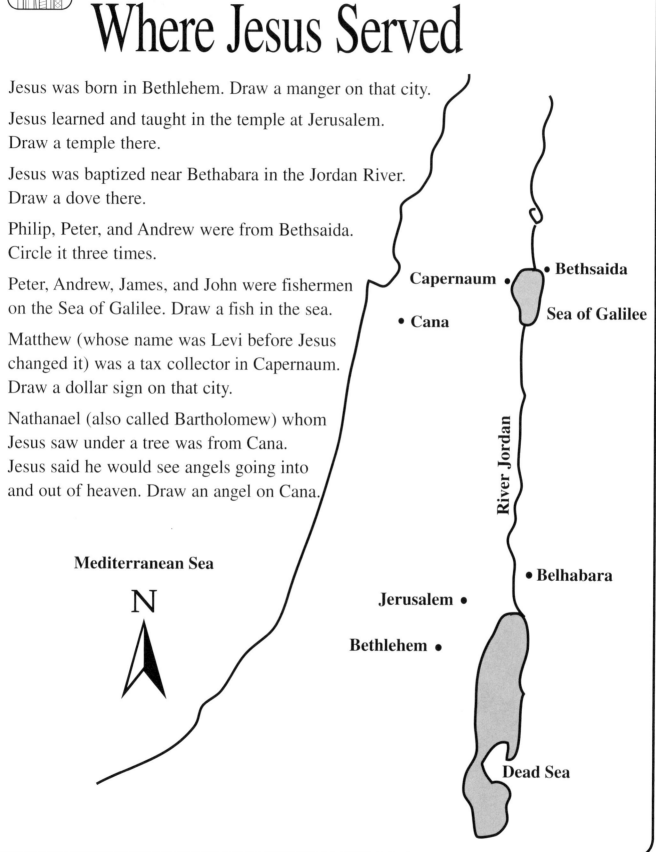

Capernaum •

• Bethsaida

• Cana

Sea of Galilee

River Jordan

Mediterranean Sea

N

• Belhabara

Jerusalem •

Bethlehem •

Dead Sea

# Jesus at the Temple

Like the other twelve-year-old boys in His town, Jesus went to Jerusalem for the Passover Feast. Unlike most twelve-year-old boys, Jesus—who was God's Son—was comfortable talking to the teachers at the temple.

*Read the story and solve the math problems in it. Then write the words before the math problems in the correct blanks to find what you can learn from the story.*

Every year Mary and Joseph went to Jerusalem for the Feast of the Passover. When Jesus (17-14= ) was twelve, His family went to (13-7= ) Jerusalem again, and this time Jesus went with them.

When they were ready to return to Nazareth, Mary and (7+2= ) Joseph thought Jesus was with the other people in their group. They traveled for a day, and then began asking (5+5= ) if anyone had seen Jesus. When Mary and Joseph couldn't find Jesus, they went back to Jerusalem to look for Him.

After three days they found Jesus sitting in the temple with the religious teachers (7+1= ) all around Him. He was listening (11-6= ) to them and asking them questions. (6+5= ) Everyone who heard Him was amazed by (1+3= ) His understanding and answers.

Mary said, "Son, why have You treated us like (14-12= ) this? Your (4+3= ) father and I have been looking for You, and we're really upset."

Jesus said, "Why were you looking for Me? Didn't you know I had to be (20-19= ) in My Father's house?"

At the time, Mary and Joseph didn't understand that Jesus was talking about (9+3= ) God (13-0= ) the Father. But Mary remembered what Jesus had said.

Something you can learn from this story:

$\underline{\quad}\ \underline{\quad}\ \underline{\quad}\ \underline{\quad}\ \underline{\quad}$
   1        2        3        4        5

$\underline{\quad}\ \underline{\quad}\ \underline{\quad}\ \underline{\quad}\ \underline{\quad}$
   6     7         8         9       10

$\underline{\quad}\ \underline{\quad}\ \underline{\quad}\ \underline{\quad}.$
      11          12       13

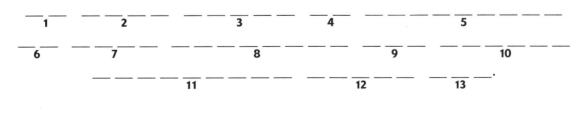

☐ *Draw a star in this box when you've read Luke 2:41-50.*

# Now Is the Time to Study Scripture

The story about Jesus at the temple shows that Jesus didn't wait until He was grown up to start learning about the Scriptures. Now is a great time for you to begin studying the Bible, too.

*Decode these ways studying the Bible can help you. Write the first letter of each picture in the blank below it.*

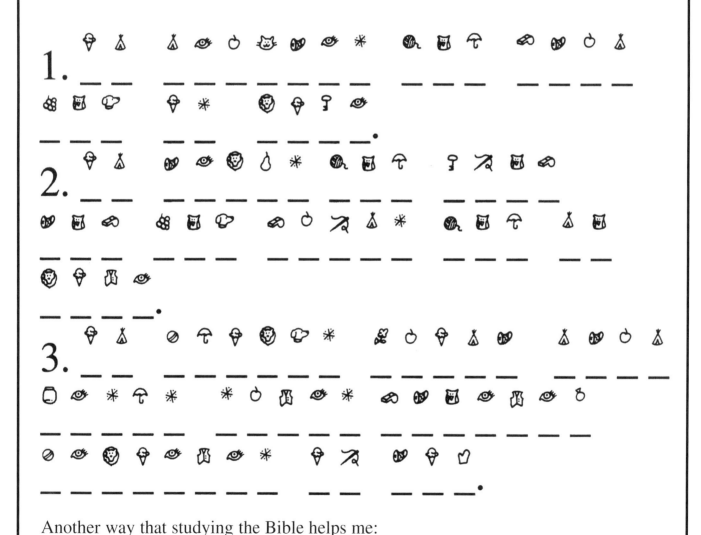

Another way that studying the Bible helps me:

_____

# John the Baptist

*Match the facts about John the Baptist with the statements about what you can learn from John's life. Then put the letters in the blanks in the correct order to discover what John the Baptist told people about Jesus' coming to earth the first time. It's a good message for us, too, because Jesus is coming again.*

1. John the Baptist's birth was a miracle because his parents (Zechariah and Elizabeth) were too old to have children. Luke 1:7

2. John the Baptist told people to repent and get ready for Jesus' coming. Matthew 3:2, 3

3. John the Baptist lived alone in the desert for a long time. Luke 1:80

4. People came to John the Baptist and confessed their sins. John baptized them in the Jordan River. He also baptized Jesus. Matthew 3:6, 13

5. John said he wasn't worthy to untie Jesus' shoes. Mark 1:7; Luke 3:16

6. John baptized with water, but he said Jesus would baptize with the Holy Spirit. Mark 1:8, Luke 3:16

7. John said that if a person had two coats, he should give one away to someone who doesn't have one. He said if a person had food to eat, he should share that, too. Luke 3:11

E. We should share what we have with others who have less.

A. When we realize how great Jesus is, we become humble and we depend on Him.

P. Even if something seems impossible, we can trust God to carry out His plans.

P. God wants us to tell Him we're sorry for what we do wrong, and ask Him to forgive us.

R. Because Jesus is coming again, we should tell others to trust Jesus so they will be ready for His coming.

E. When God asks us to do something, we can trust Him and obey Him even if it seems difficult or unusual.

R. If you believe in Jesus, He will give you the Holy Spirit to guide you.

The Message: \_\_\_\_ \_\_\_\_ \_\_\_\_ \_\_\_\_ \_\_\_\_ \_\_\_\_ \_\_\_\_
　　　　　　　　1　　2　　3　　4　　5　　6　　7

# Make a Locust to Eat

John the Baptist spent a lot of time alone in the wilderness praying to prepare for his ministry. He wore clothes made of camel's hair, and he ate locusts (grasshoppers with short antennae). Sometimes he fasted (went without food and drink). Would you fast if your mom put locusts in your lunch box? Here are some locusts that won't make you lose your appetite.

## What You Need

- thoroughly washed celery stalk
- plastic knife
- spreadable cream cheese
- 2 raisins (for eyes)
- 1 potato chip (for wings)
- toothpick
- 2 very thin pieces of carrot that are each 1" long (for antennae)

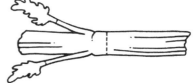

## What You Do

1. *Cut the celery stalk as shown.*
2. *Bend the thin branches to form legs.*
3. *Fill the underside with cream cheese.*
4. *Use cream cheese to paste raisins on the sides of the head.*
5. *Cut two small wings from the potato chip. Use cream cheese to paste them to the locust's back.*
6. *Use a toothpick to poke two holes in the top of the locust's head.*
7. *Push the carrot antennae into the holes.*
8. *Play with your locust and then pretend you're John the Baptist and eat it.*

*To find another food John the Baptist ate, change each letter to the letter that follows it in the alphabet.*

V H K C
G N M D X

# The Baptism of Jesus

*Jesus wanted people to know that He followed God. Read this story about a meeting between Jesus and John the Baptist.*

W +  was about 30 y +

old,  went 2  2  baptized

N the Jordan  .  said, "

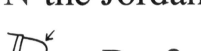 + D 2 do -B T+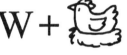 is

-L+R." W+   out of the

 , the Spirit of God came  like

a  on  .

The voice of God said, "This is My

 .    and am very

pleased with Him."

☐ *Draw a star in this box when you've read Matthew 3:13-17; Mark 1:9-11; Luke 3:21, 22; and John 1:29-34.*

# John the Baptist Crossword Puzzle

John the Baptist prepared the way for Jesus, telling people to repent and be baptized. John called Jesus the Lamb of God who would take away the sins of the world.

## ACROSS

1. Before John was born, he_____for joy inside his mother (Elizabeth) when she greeted Mary (Jesus' mother). Luke 1:44

4. John the Baptist ate wild_____. Mark 1:6

5. John's father was a priest named_____. Luke 1:5

9. John's parents were very_____when he was born. Luke 1:18

10. John told people to _____(get ready) for the coming of the Lord. Luke 3:4

12. An angel visited John's father (Zechariah) in the_____. Luke 1:9, 11

14. King_____ordered John's head to be cut off. Matt. 14:6-10

16. John_____Jesus. Luke 3:21

19. John said he wasn't good enough to untie Jesus'_____. Mark 1:7; Luke 3:16; John 1:27

21. John baptized people with_____. Luke 3:16

22. When an angel told Zechariah he would have a son, Zechariah wanted proof. The angel said he wouldn't_____ until the baby was born. Luke 1:20

## DOWN

2. John's mother was_____. Luke 1:57

3. John lived in the_____. Matt. 3:11

4. A girl who danced for King Herod asked for the_____of John the Baptist on a tray. Matt. 14:11; Mark 6:28

6. John encouraged people to_____from their sins. Matt. 3:2

7. John said Jesus would baptize with the_____. Matt. 3:11

8. John said people should give to those in_____. Luke 3:11

11. The Old Testament_____Isaiah had talked about John the Baptist long before John was born. Matt. 3:3

13. When John's message made the king angry, he threw John into _____. Mark 1:14

15. Elizabeth (John's mother) was the_____of Mary (Jesus' mother). Luke 1:36

17. An_____told Zechariah that his wife would have a baby and they should name it John. Luke 1:13

18. John baptized Jesus in the_____River. Mark 1:9

20. John told people to repent of their_____and be baptized so God could forgive them. Mark 1:4

# Jesus' Baptism and Mine

Jesus said He was baptized to "fulfill all righteousness"—to do everything that is right with God. He wants those who follow Him to be baptized. In fact, Jesus' disciples baptized more people than John the Baptist did.

Would you like to accept Jesus and become one of His followers? If so, pray a prayer like this in your own words.

Dear God,

I believe Jesus died for my sins so I can be forgiven and live with You in heaven. I'm sorry for the wrong things I've done. I trust You to forgive me because of Jesus and to help me follow You all of my life.

In Jesus' Name. Amen.

If you prayed these things and meant them, God has saved you from punishment for your sins and made you part of His family because you believe in Jesus. He will help you follow Him, and you will live with Him forever after you die. If you would like to be baptized, talk to the person who gave you this page or book.

## Jesus' Baptism

## My Baptism

*Draw a picture of your baptism the way it already happened or will happen.*

☐ *Draw a star in this box when you've read Matthew 3:15; 28:19; Mark 16:16; John 4:1, 2; and Romans 6:4.*

# The Holy Spirit Like a Dove

After Jesus was baptized, the Holy Spirit came on Him like a dove (see Matthew 3:16; Mark 1:10; Luke 3:22; and John 1:32). The Holy Spirit came to prepare Jesus for the work He was to do. The dove was a picture of the gentleness and purity of the Holy Spirit.

*Make an origami dove to remind you of Jesus' baptism.*

## What You Need

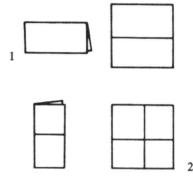

- a piece of white typing paper cut into a square
- glue
- 2 sequins or beads
- salt or silver glitter
- needle and thread

## What You Do

1. *Fold the square in half, and then open it. (Figure 1)*
2. *Fold the square in half again. When you open it, you should have four equal squares. (Figure 2)*
3. *Fold each corner toward the center. (Figure 3)*
4. *Without unfolding the square, turn it so the cross shape made by the flaps looks like an "x" shape. (Figure 4)*
5. *Fold the top left and bottom left corners so they meet in the middle. (Figure 5)*
6. *Fold the top section down so the flaps are all on the inside. (Figure 6)*
7. *Fold the left tip down to form a beak. (Figure 7)*
8. *Cut out a section as shown in Figure 7.*
9. *Fold a wing up. Turn the bird over and fold up the other wing. (Figure 8)*
10. *Glue a sequin on each side for an eye.*
11. *Outline the dove and wing with glue. Sprinkle with salt or silver glitter. Let dry.*
12. *Use the needle to poke a hole in the dove's back and push a thread through it.*
13. *Knot the thread, and hang the dove from your bedroom ceiling.*

*Draw a star in this box when you've read Matthew 3:16; Mark 1:10; Luke 3:22; and John 1:32.*

# Temptation Traps

Right after Jesus was baptized, He went into the desert. He was there for forty days, and during that time Satan tempted Him. Jesus depended on God and His Word to help Him not give in to Satan's temptations. We, too, can rely on God's Word when we're tempted to do wrong.

| | | |
|---|---|---|
| After Jesus was baptized, He fasted (prayed and didn't eat) for forty days and nights. Jesus was hungry and the devil tempted Him to turn rocks into bread. Jesus quoted from an Old Testament Scripture that said, people should not live by just eating bread; they should live by every word God says. | Next the devil took Jesus to the highest point of the temple and said, "If You are the Son of God, throw Yourself down." He quoted a psalm that said angels would catch Jesus. Jesus also quoted from an Old Testament verse that said not to test God. | Next the devil took Jesus up onto a high mountain and showed all the kingdoms of the world. The devil said, "I'll give You all these things if You fall down and worship Me." Jesus said, "Away from Me, Satan! For it is written: Worship the Lord your God, and serve Him only." Then the devil left and angels helped Jesus. |
| #1 TEMPTATION: | #2 TEMPTATION: | #3 TEMPTATION: |
| Feed your body's appetites instead of your spirit. | Do something God has forbidden to test whether God will let the natural results happen. | Do something God has forbidden to test whether God will let the natural results happen. |
| SCRIPTURE USED TO FIGHT BACK | SCRIPTURE USED TO FIGHT BACK | SCRIPTURE USED TO FIGHT BACK |
| Jesus used Deuteronomy 8:3: God says you should obey Him rather than just giving your body what it wants. | Jesus used Deuteronomy 6:16: God says you should not test Him (to see whether He'll let harm come to you when do something wrong). | Jesus used Deuteronomy 6:13: God says you should worship and serve Him only. |

# Temptation Traps (continued)

The devil tries to tempt us in the same ways he tried to tempt Jesus.
*Read these temptations, and then circle the number that describes the kind of temptation it is and how you can fight it. (See the chart on page 98 for the numbers.)*

1. "Take that comic book. If you get caught, God will always forgive you."　　　1　　2　　3

2. "You're starving. Go ahead and eat your brother's candy bar."　　　1　　2　　3

3. "The cashier gave you too much change. Keep it anyway."　　　1　　2　　3

4. "Watch that movie. You'll forget the bad parts."　　　1　　2　　3

5. "You're too tired to go to church. Stay in bed instead."　　　1　　2　　3

6. "You can make lots of friends by helping them cheat on the exam."　　　1　　2　　3

7. "Make a joke about the unpopular girl. People will think you're funny."　　　1　　2　　3

8. "Don't give your offering. You'll have more money to spend on yourself."　　　1　　2　　3

9. "Take these drugs. They won't hurt you."　　　1　　2　　3

10. "People will like you more if they don't know you're a Christian."　　　1　　2　　3

☐ *Draw a star in this box when you've read Matthew 4:1-11; Mark 1:12; and Luke 4:1-13.*

# Fight Back with the Word of God

Because Jesus was God's Son, He never did anything wrong (Hebrews 4:15). Jesus does, however, know what it is like to be tempted to do wrong. But He didn't give in when Satan tried to get Him to sin. Jesus fought back with the Word of God. You can fight back the same way when you're tempted to do wrong things.

Like soldiers who, in ancient times, wore armor into battle, Ephesians 6:11 says to put on the full armor of God so you can fight the devil. Verse 17 says to fight with the sword of the Spirit, which is the Word of God.

What is something you're tempted to do, even though you know it's wrong? Find a Bible verse you can use to fight against that temptation. (If you can't find one yourself, ask a grown-up for help.) Make the sword pictured below as a reminder to use God's Word when you're fighting temptation. When you are tempted, quote that particular verse to help you say no to temptation.

## Make a Sword of the Spirit

### What You Need

- large piece of heavy cardboard
- pencil
- scissors
- paper cup
- masking tape
- silver spray paint or aluminum foil

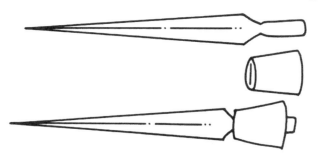

### What You Do

*1. Draw a sword like the one pictured here on the cardboard, and cut it out.*

*2. Poke a hole in the bottom of the cup, and insert it onto the sword. Tape it in place. Cut a slit on each side of the cup so it will fit over your hand.*

*3. Spray paint the sword silver or cover it with aluminum foil.*

Keep the sword in your bedroom. Each time you see it or play with it, practice memorizing the Bible verse you chose to fight temptation. When you are tempted to sin, quote the verse and ask God's help in resisting temptation.

# Andrew

*Match each paragraph to its picture. Write the number of the paragraph above the picture. After you read the paragraphs, think about your answers to the questions.*

**1.** One day as Andrew listened to John the Baptist preach, Jesus walked by them. "Look!" John the Baptist said. "The Lamb of God." Andrew and another person followed Jesus. Jesus turned around and asked, "What are you looking for?"

"Teacher," they asked, "where are You staying?"

"Come and see," Jesus replied. So Andrew went with Jesus and stayed with Him from about 4:00 p.m. until evening. If you could have spent an afternoon with Jesus while He lived on earth, what would you have asked Him?

**A**

**2.** Andrew left Jesus and told his brother Peter that he had found the Messiah. Andrew then brought Peter to Jesus. The two brothers were fishermen and they lived in the town of Bethsaida. One day Jesus was walking beside the Sea of Galilee and He saw Andrew and Peter fishing. Jesus called to them, "Come, follow Me, and I will make you fishers of men." They immediately left their nets and followed Him. How can people be fishers of men? Who can you tell about Jesus?

**B**

**3.** One time as Jesus left the temple, someone pointed out to Him how magnificent the temple was. Jesus said, "Do you see all these great buildings? One day not one stone here will be left on the ground." Peter, James, John, and Andrew asked Jesus when all these things would happen. Jesus told them what the world would be like before He returned. He said no one would know exactly when He was coming back. Are you watching for Jesus? Do you know some of the things that will happen before He comes?

**C**

**4.** Another day when Jesus was teaching, He asked His disciples how they were going to feed the crowd that had gathered to listen. There were more than 5,000 people. Andrew told Him about a boy that had five loaves of bread and two small fish. Andrew said, "But how far will that go?" Andrew watched Jesus take the bread and fish, thank God for the food, and divide it up. Miraculously it was enough to feed all of the people with twelve baskets left over. Jesus can do anything, even things that seem impossible. Is there something you need Him to do?

**D**

*Draw a star in this box when you've read Matthew 4:18-22; Mark 1:16-18; 13:1-4, 35; and John 1:35-42; 6:8-13.*

# Andrew—A Good Brother

Andrew was a good brother to Simon Peter because He told Him about Jesus. Are you a good brother or sister? Do you talk to your brothers and sisters about Jesus and help them follow Him?

*Unscramble each of these ways you can be a good brother or sister by helping family members learn about and follow Jesus. Circle the things that you do often.*

1. daeR het lebiB getotehr.

2. leTl hemt wsya taht Gdo sanwres oyur yarpsre.

3. lelT hetm hewn uyo rea rosyr os ti si seaire fro emht ot rofgvie ouy.

4. loFlow het logned lure dan retta hetm sa uoy nwat ot eb dateret.

5. howS nda letl htme uyo veol meth.

6. yarP rof tehm.

# Simon Peter

The pictures on this page will help you complete this story about Peter, one of Jesus' disciples.

*Write the answer in each blank and put the correct number next to each picture. Number one has been done for you.*

1.

Andrew told his brother Simon about Jesus. Jesus renamed Simon Cephas, or Peter, which meant "rock." One day Peter was throwing a 1. <u>net</u> into the sea when Jesus walked by. Jesus told Peter and Andrew they would become fishers of 2. _____ if they followed Him.

Peter saw Jesus perform many miracles. When Peter's mother-in-law was sick, her fever left when Jesus touched her 3. _____. Another time Jesus walked on a 4. _____. Peter tried to walk on the water to Jesus, but when he saw the wild wind, Peter became afraid and started to 5. _____. When Jesus took Peter, James, and John up a mountain one day, Jesus changed so that his face was shining like the 6. _____. A bright 7. _____ overshadowed them and a voice called out, "This is My Son, whom I love; I am very pleased with Him. Listen to Him!"

Once when they needed to pay temple taxes, Jesus sent Peter to find a coin in the mouth of a 8. _____. Peter, James, and John saw Jesus bring a twelve-year-old 9. _____ back to life.

When Jesus asked the disciples who they said He was, Peter said, "You are the Christ, the Son of the living God." Jesus told Peter He would give him the 10. _____ of the kingdom of heaven. Another time Peter asked Jesus what he and the other disciples would have for leaving everything and following Him. Jesus said they would each sit on a 11. _____ and judge the 12. ____ tribes of Israel.

Jesus taught Peter and the other disciples great truths. One day Peter asked how often to forgive someone who did something wrong against him. Jesus said he should forgive 13. ____ times.

Peter told Jesus he was ready to go with Jesus to 14. _____ and to death. When the Jewish leaders came to take Jesus away, Peter cut off Malchus's 15. _____ , but Jesus healed it. After Jesus was arrested, Peter denied the Lord and told 16. __ different people he wasn't Jesus' follower. When he heard the 17. _____ crow and Jesus looked at him, Peter 18. _____. He repented and later wrote letters that became books of the 19._____ called I Peter and II Peter.

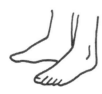 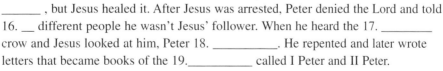    

*Draw a star in this box when you've read Matthew 5:18-19; 8:15; 14:30, 35; 16:16-19; 17:2-3, 5; 19:27-28 Mark 5:42; Luke 22:33; 23:62; and John 1:40, 42; 18:10.*

# Peter, the Rock

When Jesus met Simon, He changed Simon's name to Peter, which meant "rock." He knew someday Simon would become a person whose faith in Jesus was unshakable like a rock. Peter didn't start out that way, but later his faith grew strong enough that he was able to become a great leader of the early Christian church.

*Make some rock candy or a pebble person to remind you of the meaning of Peter's name. When you pray today, ask God to help you see yourself the way He wants you to become.*

## Rock Candy

### What You Need

- a tall, narrow jar
- a pencil or Popsicle stick
- a clean piece of string
- a paper clip
- a saucepan
- 1 cup granulated sugar
- 1/2 cup water
- a drop of food color

### What You Do

1. *Tie one end of the string to the pencil or stick. Tie the other end to the paper clip. Lay the pencil or stick across the top of the jar, and drop the paper clip into the jar.*
2. *Pour the sugar and water into the saucepan. Stir the mixture constantly over low heat. When it begins to boil, keep stirring until the mixture has boiled for two more minutes. Then carefully pour the mixture into the jar.*
3. *After mixture cools, put the jar where it won't be bumped.*
4. *Carefully skim the crystals off the surface of the water once or twice each day so the water can keep evaporating.*
5. *After about a week, pull the string of candy out of the water, rinse it off, and eat it.*

### What You Need

- a small, round rock for a head, a medium rock for a body, a large rock for a base, and four long rocks for arms and legs
- tacky glue (found in craft stores)
- fabric scraps
- acrylic paints

## A Pebble Man

### What You Do

1. *Wash the rocks and let them dry.*
2. *Glue the rocks together with tacky glue to make the pebble person.*
3. *When dry, glue on fabric scraps for clothes and let them dry. Paint Simon Peter with acrylic paints.*

# James and John 'Sons of Thunder'

*Find ten words that are hidden in the picture. Circle them and then write them in the blanks where they belong in the story.*

James and John were _____, sons of a man named Zebedee. They were _____ on the Sea of Galilee and were partners with Simon Peter and Andrew. One day when they were _____ their fishing nets, Jesus came up to them and said, "Follow Me." They left their nets and _____ Him.

Two different times Jesus amazed James and John by miraculously filling nets with _____. Once there were so many that the net broke and their boat almost sank. Another time the net was so full that they couldn't lift it; they had to drag it behind their boat.

Jesus called James and John "Boanerges," which means "sons of _____." There could be so many reasons for that nickname. Perhaps it is because they were bold and unafraid to tell people about Jesus.

Peter, James, and John had a special closeness with Jesus. Sometimes Jesus shared experiences that were very special with just the three of them. One of those times was when Jesus was "transfigured"–His _____ shone like the sun, His clothes became as white as light, and a voice from heaven said, "This is My beloved Son."

John wrote the books in the Bible titled John, I John, II John, III John, and the _____. He called himself "the disciple whom Jesus loved." Of course Jesus loved all of the disciples, but John must have felt that the most important thing about himself was Jesus' love for him. When Jesus was dying on the cross, He asked John to take care of Mary as if she were John's own _____.

*Draw a star in this box when you've read Matthew 4:21-22; 17:1; Mark 1:19-20; 3:17; 9:2; Luke 5:3-11; 9:28; and John 19:26; 21:1-24.*

# Egg Fish

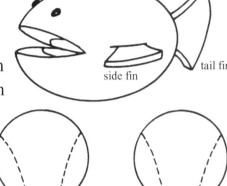

back fin

side fin        tail fin

Make an egg fish to remind you of James and John because they were mending their fishing nets when Jesus said, "Follow Me," and twice Jesus miraculously filled their nets with fish.

## What You Need

- a peeled, boiled egg
- a thin cucumber or zucchini slice to make a tail fin
- three thin carrot or radish slices to make back and side fins
- two cloves for eyes
- a plastic knife

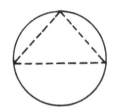

Carrot or Radish slice (side fins)

## What You Do

1. *Cut a mouth from one end of the egg.*
2. *Poke cloves above it for eyes.*
3. *Cut a small slit on the fish's back, a small slit on each side, and a slit on the tail end.*
4. *Cut the vegetable slices as shown at right, and insert them into the egg's slits.*

Carrot or Radish slice (back fin)

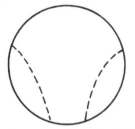

Cucumber or Zucchini slice (tail fin)

# What John Called Himself

Write the first letter after the dot in the first blank below. Skip a letter and write the next letter in the next blank below. Continue skipping a letter and writing a letter until you reach the dot. Skip the first letter after the dot. Write the next letter. Continue skipping a letter and writing a letter until you reach the dot again. You will see what John called himself.

___  _____  _____  _____

# Philip, the Good Friend

*Correct the spacing, and read this story about Philip who brought one of his friends to Jesus. The first line is done for you.*

Phi lip|was|fro m|Beth sai da,|the|same|ci ty|as|Pe ter|and|And rew.|One|day|Je sus|fo und|
Phi lipin Ga lil eeandsaid, "Fol low Me." Phi lipfo undNa than ae land said, "Weha vefo undthe oneMo sesand thepro phets wro tea bout, Je susof Na zare th, theso nofJo seph."

Phi liplo ved hisfr ien denough toloo kfor himso heco uld tellhim a bout Je sus. Doyou ha vea fri end whois n't a Chri sti anyet? Ifyo u ha vegi ven yourli fe tothe Lord, tellyour fri endabo utit. Ex plain thatJesusloves usso mu chthat Hediedsowe canbe for givenof whatwe dowro n gand livewi thGod; we jus thave toask Himto beour Savior. Ifyour fri endwa nts Je susto save-him or her, he lpyo urfriend prayabo utit.

Ifyo uand yourfri end haveaccepted Jes us, you havebeen adop ted into thefam ilyof God, andnow youare bro thersor sist ers!

# Make Peanut Puppet Friends

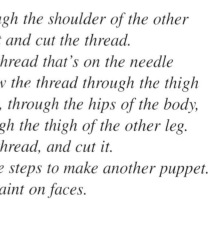

*Act out Philip telling Nathanael about Jesus, or pretend that you're telling your friend about Jesus.*

## What You Need

• *12 peanuts in shells (extras for snacking)* • *scissors*
• *a darning needle and strong thread* • *markers or paints*

## What You Do

1. *Thread the needle and tie a knot in the thread.*
2. *Sew the head to the body as shown. Leave the knot hanging loose so you can tie the two ends together when you've threaded the needle through the peanut. Tie the ends and cut the thread.*
3. *Knot the thread that's on the needle. Sew the thread through the shoulder of one arm, then through the chest of the body,* *then through the shoulder of the other arm. Knot and cut the thread.*
4. *Knot the thread that's on the needle again. Sew the thread through the thigh of one leg, through the hips of the body, and through the thigh of the other leg. Knot the thread, and cut it.*
5. *Repeat the steps to make another puppet.*
6. *Draw or paint on faces.*

☐ *Draw a star in this box when you've read the story in John 1:35-46.*

# Nathanael

When Jesus saw Nathanael coming with Philip, Jesus said, "Here is an Israelite . . . in whom there is nothing false!" Jesus was saying that Nathanael was honest and that he never tried to trick people into believing something that wasn't true. Nathanael asked, "How do you know me?" Jesus answered, "Before Philip came to you, I saw you under a fig tree."

Nathanael said, "You are the Son of God! Truly, You are the King of Israel!"

Jesus said, "You believe because I told you I saw you under the fig tree. You shall see greater things than that." Then He said Nathanael would see heaven open and the angels of God going up from Jesus and coming down to Him.

It is likely that Nathanael was the disciple called Bartholomew in the books of Matthew, Mark, and Luke.

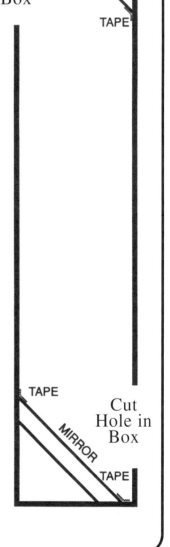

## Make a Periscope

Jesus saw Nathanael sitting under a tree before Nathanael had ever met Jesus. Even though you can't see God, He's watching all the time. Remembering that God is watching over you can help you when you're afraid or needing to say no to doing wrong things.

Make this periscope to remind you that God watches over you always.

## What You Need

- a tall, narrow box
- 2 small mirrors
- scissors or a plastic knife
- strong tape

## What You Do

1. Cut holes in the box as shown in the illustration.
2. Slant the mirrors in front of the holes as shown, and tape in place.
3. Hide behind a large object. Look through the bottom hole of your periscope. You should be able to see what is in front of the top hole.

Draw a star in this box when you've read the story in John 1:47-51.

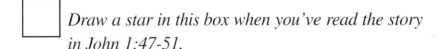

# Thomas, the Twin

*Cross out the twin words and read the story. The first one is done for you.*

One of the disciples was called ~~Thomas~~ Thomas (he was also called Didymus). Both names mean mean "twin." People today don't usually think think of this disciple as "the twin," they think of him as "Doubting Thomas." Have Have you ever ever heard someone called called a doubting Thomas? Sometimes people call someone that that if the person doesn't seem to have much faith. faith.

After Jesus rose from the dead dead, He visited the disciples, but Thomas Thomas wasn't there. When the other disciples disciples told him about it, he said he he wouldn't believe unless he saw the prints of the nails nails in Jesus' hands and put his finger finger into them as well as the wound in Jesus' side. side.

Do you believe Jesus is alive? If you believe, He is the Son of God, and that He died for your sins, and rose from the dead, color in these hands and write "I believe" with a red marker or crayon inside the wounded hands.

A week, later later Jesus appeared appeared to the disciples again. This time time Thomas was there, and Jesus let Thomas touch touch His hands and side. Then He said, "Stop doubting and believe." Thomas said, "My Lord Lord and my God." Jesus Jesus said, "Thomas, you believed believed because you you have have seen seen Me. Me. Blessed Blessed are those who have believed without seeing seeing."

John said these things were written written so you might believe Jesus is the Christ, Christ, the Son of the living living God, and that because you believe, you can live live again. This story story comes from John 20:24-31.

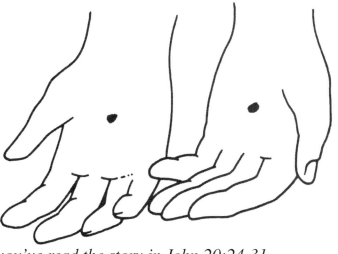

| | Draw a star in this box when you've read the story in John 20:24-31.

# A Doubting and Believing Cup Puppet

How do you think Thomas felt before and after he saw for himself that Jesus was alive? *Make this puppet to remind you that God wants you to be a believer.*

## What You Need

- 2 plain paper cups
- permanent markers
- scissors or a plastic knife

## What You Do

1. *On the side of a cup, draw a face without a mouth on it. Cut slots as shown in the drawing—one where the mouth should be and one for a word to show through.*
2. *Put the second cup inside the first one. Draw a smile in the mouth slot. Write the word "believing" in the word slot. Turn cup two to the other side, and draw a frown in the mouth slot and write the word "doubting" in the word slot. Use the puppet to tell the story about Thomas.*

Cut out openings

Outer Cup

Inner Cup (front)

Inner Cup (back)

# Thomas was Devoted

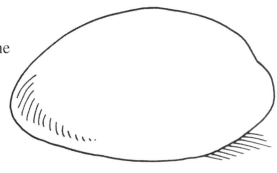

Most people remember Thomas for doubting, but he also had great courage and devotion to the Lord. Some Jews in Jerusalem wanted to kill Jesus. When Jesus said He was going to return there, Thomas was willing to follow Jesus even though he thought he might be killed. Thomas said to the other disciples, "Let's go that we may die with Him."

Find a smooth rock. Use a marker and write this question on it: Would I follow Jesus even if I thought I might be killed? Think about your answer.

*Draw a star in this box when you've read the story in John 11:7-16.*

# Matthew, the Tax Collector

*As you find each word in the maze, fill in the blanks and read about Matthew. Would you be willing to leave everything behind and follow Jesus like Matthew did? If you need help, look up the Bible verses for the correct words.*

Matthew was a _____, for the Roman leaders. He was at _____ collecting taxes when _____ saw him. Jesus said, "_____ Me," and Matthew _____ up and followed Jesus (Matthew 9:9). Later Jesus called Matthew to become one of His twelve _____ (Matthew 10:2-3).

Matthew wrote the first book in the New Testament, the Gospel of Matthew. Matthew is also called _____ (Mark 2:14). Matthew's _____ was Alphaeus (Matthew 2:14).

After Jesus returned to _____, Matthew was one of the followers who gathered and waited for the Holy Spirit to come (Acts 1:13).

WORK
JESUS
LEVI
TAX COLLECTOR
DISCIPLES
FOLLOW
HEAVEN
WORK
JESUS
FOLLOW
START HERE
STOOD
JESUS
FINISH HERE
FATHER
JESUS
DISCIPLES
FATHER
TAX COLLECTOR
WORK
HEAVEN
FOLLOW
LEVI
STOOD

# Same-Named Apostles

Even though Jesus called twelve very different men to be His apostles, some of them had the same names. These names were James, Simon, and Judas. Each of these names was shared by a pair of apostles. Read about these same-named apostles.

## James
There were two apostles named James. One was a fisherman who was John's brother and Zebedee's son. He is called James the Greater. James the Younger was the son of Alphaeus. James the Younger's mother, Mary, was one of the women who first came to Jesus' tomb after He had died.

## Simon
There were two apostles named Simon. One was Andrew's brother whom Jesus renamed Peter. The other Simon was called Simon the Zealot. Before this Simon followed Jesus, he belonged to a group called the Zealots who didn't want the Romans to rule over the Jews.

## Judas
There were two apostles named Judas. One was Judas Iscariot, who betrayed Jesus by turning Him over to the Jewish leaders who wanted to kill Him. The other Judas was the son of James.

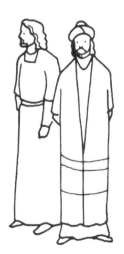

Judas, the son of James, once asked Jesus an important question: "Why will you show yourself to us (the apostles) and not the world?" Jesus said, "If anyone loves me, he will obey my teaching. My Father will love him, and we will come to him and make our home with him" (John 14:22, 23).

Sometimes Judas was called Thaddaeus.

# Make a Pennant

These apostles loved and followed Jesus. Make this pennant to announce your love for Jesus.

## What You Need

- a piece of light-colored felt, cut in a triangle
- pencil
- black fabric marker or fabric paint
- dowel or stick
- stapler
- glue and glitter, optional

## What You Do

1. *Lightly write "I Love Jesus" on the felt with the pencil. Be sure to leave a 2-inch margin along side A.*
2. *Cover the pencil marks with fabric marker or fabric paint.*
3. *Wrap the edge of side A around the dowel. Hold the edge against the pennant and slip out the dowel.*
4. *Staple the edge to the pennant, forming a tube along side A.*
5. *Slip the dowel back into the tube.*
6. *Decorate the pennant with glitter, if you'd like.*

# Judas Iscariot, the Betrayer

Some people wonder why Jesus chose Judas Iscariot to be a disciple. Since Jesus knew what was going to happen to Him—including Judas's betrayal—why didn't He choose someone else as a disciple? The Bible doesn't tell us why Jesus chose Judas, only that Jesus loved Judas Iscariot and was deeply saddened when Judas betrayed Him. *Follow the code to fill in the missing letters and read the story.*

| CODE | |
|---|---|
| #1 blanks = U | #6 blanks = B |
| #2 blanks = O | #7 blanks = D |
| #3 blanks = I | #8 blanks = R |
| #4 blanks = E | #9 blanks = S |
| #5 blanks = A | #10 blanks = T |

J_ _ _ _ _ _c_ _ _ _ _ carried the money for
  1 7 5 9  3 9 5 8 3 2 0

the other _p_ _ _l_ _ and J_ _ _ _ _. He
    5 2 9 0 4 9    4 9 1 9

often _ _ _l_ from the m_n_y _ _g.
   9 0 2 4      2 4  6 5

Judas went to the Jewish l_ _ _ _ _ _ and made a
                4 5 7 4 8 9

_ _ _l with them to help them c_ _ch Jesus. They
7 4 5             5 0

paid Judas _h_ _ _y p_ _c_ _ of _ _lv_ _.
      0 3 8 0  3 4 4 9    9 3 4 8

Judas _ _l_ the Jewish leaders that he w_ _l_
     0 2 7                2 1 7

let them know wh_ Jesus was by k_ _ _ _ng Him.
        2            3 9 9 3

When J_ _ _ _ kissed Jesus in the G_ _ _ _n of
     1 7 5 9          5 8 7 4

G_ _h_ _m_n_, the Jewish leaders g_ _ _ _ _ _
 4 0 9 4 5 4           8 5 6 6 4 7

Jesus and _ _ _k Him _w_y.
       0 2 2      5 5

☐ *Draw a star in this box when you've read the stories in Matthew 26:14-16; 27:5; Mark 14:32, 44-46; and John 12:6.*

# Being Loyal to Jesus

Have you heard the expression "true blue"? Being true blue means to be loyal no matter what happens. Your family is true blue because they stand by you, even when things are difficult. Judas Iscariot seemed true blue to Jesus because Judas was one of Jesus' disciples; but, in the end, Judas wasn't true blue at all. He cared more about himself than following Jesus.

*Circle the answers that show a person's "true blue" colors for Jesus. Then color the spaces of the picture using the colors you circled for each number's question.*

1. I want to try to tell people about Jesus.              Often/blue      Never/red

2. I'm embarrassed to tell people I'm a Christian.     Often/blue      Never/red

3. I listen when I pray and try to do what Jesus
   tells me to do.                                               Always/green    Never/yellow

4. My friends talk me into doing things I know
   are wrong.                                                     Often/orange    Never/purple

# Who Am I?

*Use the clues to name each of the apostles you've learned about in this book.*

1. My friend Philip brought me to Jesus. I'm __ __ __ __ __ __ __ __ __ (or Bartholomew).

2. I'm Alphaeus's son. One of the Sons of Thunder has the same name as me. I'm
__ __ __ __ __.

3. I followed John the Baptist who told about Jesus' coming. I brought my brother to Jesus. I'm __ __ __ __ __ __.

4. I'm a twin. Unfortunately most people think of me as a doubter even though I believed Jesus rose from the dead after I saw Him with my own eyes. I'm __ __ __ __ __ __.

5. For a small amount of money, I betrayed Jesus. I'm __ __ __ __ __
__ __ __ __ __ __ __ __.

6. My name was Simon but Jesus gave me a name that meant "rock." I was a great leader of the church after Jesus returned to heaven. My name is __ __ __ __ __.

7. I'm one of the Sons of Thunder. I call myself "the disciple whom Jesus loved." I'm
__ __ __ __.

8. I'm the other Son of Thunder. Peter, John, and I were with Jesus when He was transfigured and His face shone like the sun and His clothes were as white as light. I saw Moses and Elijah with Him. I'm __ __ __ __ __.

9. Right after Jesus told me to follow Him, I went to find my friend Nathanael so I could tell him about Jesus. I'm __ __ __ __ __ __ __.

10. I wrote the first book in the New Testament. I was working as a tax collector when Jesus told me to follow Him. I obeyed and left everything to follow Him. I'm
__ __ __ __ __ __ __.

11. Some call me Thaddaeus. My father's name was James. The disciple who betrayed Jesus has the same name as me. I'm __ __ __ __ __ .

12. I'm called Zealot because I belonged to a group called the Zealots that didn't want the Romans to rule over the Jews. Peter has the same first name as me. I'm __ __ __ __ __.

# Apostle Trivia Game

## What You Need

- 2-4 players
- one marker for each player (different coins or paper scraps of different colors)
- game board from page 118
- question cards from pages 119-126 (each of which may be used more than once in a game)
- dice

## How to Play

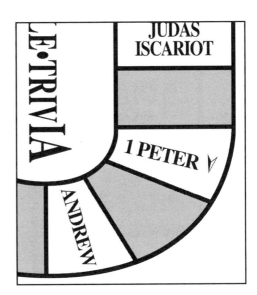

1. Players place their markers on the space that says "1 Peter." Each player rolls the dice. The player with the highest roll goes first.

2. Player one rolls again and following the arrow moves the number of spaces indicated by the dice. If he lands on an apostle space, he answers a question about that apostle. If his answer is incorrect, his turn is over. If he answers correctly, he keeps that apostle question card and rolls again. If he lands on an apostle for which he has already won a card, he rolls again.

3. The first player to collect all twelve apostle cards wins.

When the game is over, put the question cards in an envelope, and tape the envelope inside this book so you can play the game again another time.

*Cut out the cards. Keep them face-up so the answers don't show.*

**PETER**

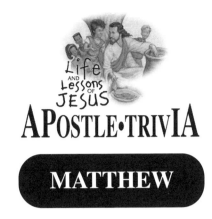

**MATTHEW**

**PHILIP**

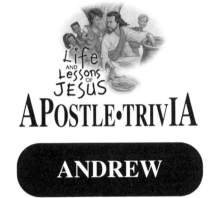

**ANDREW**

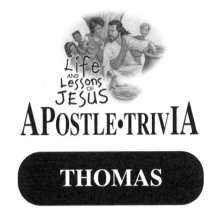

**THOMAS**

**NATHANAEL**

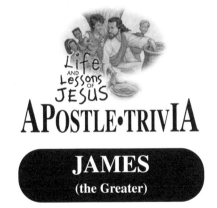

**JAMES**
(the Greater)

**JUDAS**

**SIMON**

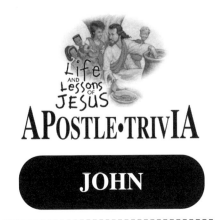

**JOHN**

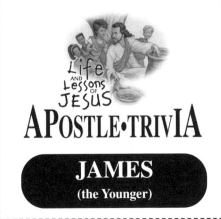

**JAMES**
(the Younger)

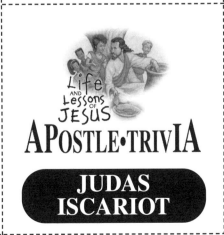

**JUDAS ISCARIOT**

## PHILIP

**Q.** I was from which city?

**A.** Bethsaida

## MATTHEW

**Q.** I am also called what name?

**A.** Levi

## PETER

**Q.** What does my name mean?

**A.** Rock

## NATHANAEL

**Q.** Who took me to meet Jesus?

**A.** Philip

## THOMAS

**Q.** I was willing to go with Jesus to heal Lazarus even though I thought this might happen.

**A.** Might be killed

## ANDREW

**Q.** Who was my brother?

**A.** Simon Peter

## SIMON

**Q.** What nickname did people give me that started with Z?

**A.** Zealot

## JUDAS

**Q.** I was also called this.

**A.** Thaddaeus

## JAMES
### (the Greater)

**Q.** What did Jesus call my brother and me?

**A.** Sons of Thunder

## JUDAS ISCARIOT

**Q.** What was in the bag I carried while traveling with Jesus and the Apostles?

**A.** Money

## JAMES
### (the Younger)

**Q.** Who was my father?

**A.** Alphaeus

## JOHN

**Q.** What did I call myself?

**A.** The disciple Jesus loved

APOSTLE·TRIVIA

**PETER**

APOSTLE·TRIVIA

**MATTHEW**

APOSTLE·TRIVIA

**PHILIP**

APOSTLE·TRIVIA

**ANDREW**

APOSTLE·TRIVIA

**THOMAS**

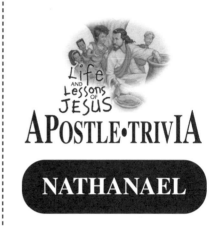

APOSTLE·TRIVIA

**NATHANAEL**

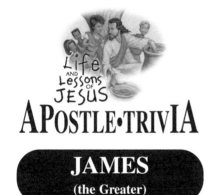

APOSTLE·TRIVIA

**JAMES**
(the Greater)

APOSTLE·TRIVIA

**JUDAS**

APOSTLE·TRIVIA

**SIMON**

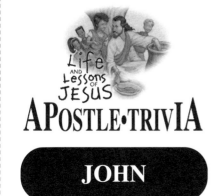

APOSTLE·TRIVIA

**JOHN**

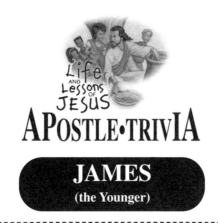

APOSTLE·TRIVIA

**JAMES**
(the Younger)

APOSTLE·TRIVIA

**JUDAS
ISCARIOT**

### PHILIP

Q. What brothers were from my home town?

A. Simon (Peter) and Andrew

### MATTHEW

Q. What was I doing when Jesus told me to follow Him?

A. Collecting taxes

### PETER

Q. Jesus said I would become a fisher of what?

A. Men

### NATHANAEL

Q. Before I met Jesus, He had seen me under a what?

A. Fig tree

### THOMAS

Q. Why wasn't I as convinced as the other apostles that Jesus had risen from the dead?

A. I wasn't there when they saw Him alive.

### ANDREW

Q. I saw Jesus feed more than 5000 people with what?

A. 5 loaves of bread and 2 fish

### SIMON

Q. Another apostle shared my name, but Jesus renamed him. What was his *new* name?

A. Peter

### JUDAS

Q. Who was my father?

A. James

### JAMES
(the Greater)

Q. My brother and I were fishermen. What was my brother's name?

A. John

### JUDAS ISCARIOT

Q. What did the Jewish leaders give me for betraying Jesus?

A. 30 pieces of silver

### JAMES
(the Younger)

Q. My mother saw Jesus after He rose from the dead. What is rising from the dead called?

A. The Resurrection

### JOHN

Q. Who did Jesus ask me to take care of when He was dying on the cross?

A. His mother, Mary

**APOSTLE·TRIVIA**

**PETER**

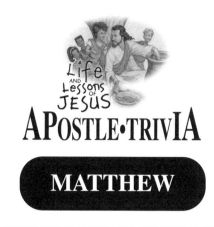

**APOSTLE·TRIVIA**

**MATTHEW**

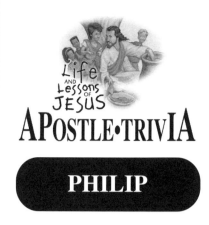

**APOSTLE·TRIVIA**

**PHILIP**

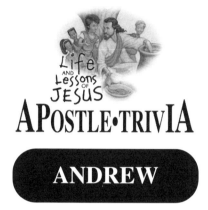

**APOSTLE·TRIVIA**

**ANDREW**

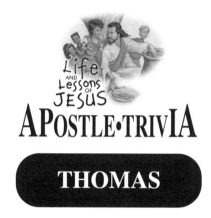

**APOSTLE·TRIVIA**

**THOMAS**

**APOSTLE·TRIVIA**

**NATHANAEL**

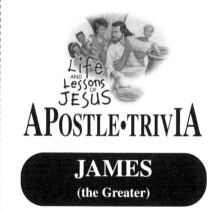

**APOSTLE·TRIVIA**

**JAMES**
(the Greater)

**APOSTLE·TRIVIA**

**JUDAS**

**APOSTLE·TRIVIA**

**SIMON**

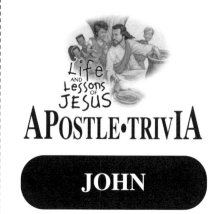

**APOSTLE·TRIVIA**

**JOHN**

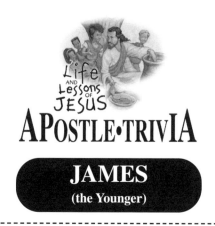

**APOSTLE·TRIVIA**

**JAMES**
(the Younger)

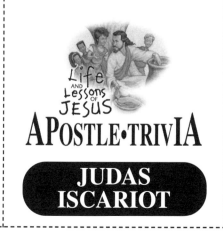

**APOSTLE·TRIVIA**

**JUDAS ISCARIOT**

## PHILIP

**Q.** Whom did I tell about Jesus?

**A.** Nathanael (Bartholomew)

## MATTHEW

**Q.** I wrote the first book in the New Testament. What is it called?

**A.** Matthew

## PETER

**Q.** How many times did Jesus say I should forgive someone?

**A.** 77 times

## NATHANAEL

**Q.** I told Jesus I knew He was the ____ of God, and the ____ of Israel.

**A.** Son / King

## THOMAS

**Q.** What did I want as proof that Jesus rose from the dead?

**A.** Put my fingers in the nail holes in His hands, and my hand into His side.

## ANDREW

**Q.** What was I doing when Jesus said to follow Him?

**A.** Fishing

## SIMON

**Q.** What was the name of the political group to which I belonged?

**A.** Zealots

## JUDAS

**Q.** What question did I ask Jesus?

**A.** "Why do you intend to show Yourself to us and not to the world?"

## JAMES
### (the Greater)

**Q.** My brother and I were fishermen with which other brothers?

**A.** Simon (Peter) and Andrew

## JUDAS ISCARIOT

**Q.** How did I let the Jewish leaders know which man was Jesus?

**A.** I kissed Him on the cheek.

## JAMES
### (the Younger)

**Q.** What two other names were shared by pairs of apostles?

**A.** Simon and Judas

## JOHN

**Q.** I wrote the last book in the New Testament. What is it called?

**A.** Revelation

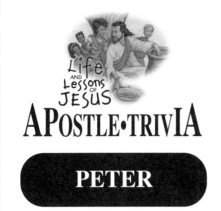

APOSTLE·TRIVIA

**PETER**

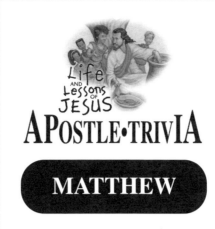

APOSTLE·TRIVIA

**MATTHEW**

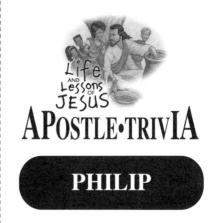

APOSTLE·TRIVIA

**PHILIP**

APOSTLE·TRIVIA

**ANDREW**

APOSTLE·TRIVIA

**THOMAS**

APOSTLE·TRIVIA

**NATHANAEL**

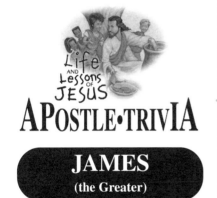

APOSTLE·TRIVIA

**JAMES**
(the Greater)

APOSTLE·TRIVIA

**JUDAS**

APOSTLE·TRIVIA

**SIMON**

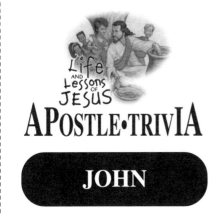

APOSTLE·TRIVIA

**JOHN**

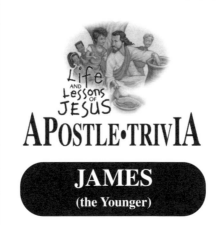

APOSTLE·TRIVIA

**JAMES**
(the Younger)

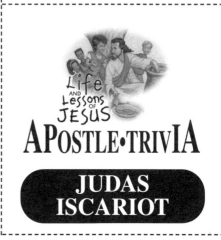

APOSTLE·TRIVIA

**JUDAS
ISCARIOT**

## PHILIP

**Q.** What did I tell Nathanael to do after I told him about Jesus?

**A.** Go and see Jesus.

## MATTHEW

**Q.** After Jesus went to heaven, I met with other believers to wait for what?

**A.** The Holy Spirit

## PETER

**Q.** I denied Jesus three times before I heard what sound?

**A.** The rooster crow

## NATHANAEL

**Q.** What did Jesus say I would see going up and down into heaven?

**A.** Angels

## THOMAS

**Q.** What do people call me because they think I don't have much faith?

**A.** Doubting Thomas

## ANDREW

**Q.** Why did Jesus say we needed to watch carefully to be ready for His return?

**A.** No one knows when it will be

## SIMON

**Q.** I didn't want which nation to rule over Israel?

**A.** Roman Empire

## JUDAS

**Q.** What did Jesus tell me people would do if they loved Him?

**A.** Obey His teaching

## JAMES
### (the Greater)

**Q.** I was a fisherman on which sea?

**A.** Sea of Galilee

## JUDAS ISCARIOT

**Q.** To where did I lead the Jewish leaders to arrest Jesus?

**A.** Garden of Gethsemane

## JAMES
### (the Younger)

**Q.** What am I called because I might be younger than the other James?

**A.** James the Younger

## JOHN

**Q.** What was my career before I met Jesus?

**A.** Fisherman

# I Did It!

| COMPLETED | DATE | COMPLETED | DATE |
|-----------|------|-----------|------|
| ☐ Palestine, Where Jesus Served | _____ | ☐ Simon Peter | _____ |
| ☐ Jesus at the Temple | _____ | ☐ Peter, the Rock | _____ |
| ☐ Now Is the Time to Study Scripture | _____ | ☐ James and John, Sons of Thunder | _____ |
| ☐ John the Baptist | _____ | ☐ Philip, the Good Friend | _____ |
| ☐ Make a Locust to Eat | _____ | ☐ Nathanael | _____ |
| ☐ The Baptism of Jesus | _____ | ☐ Thomas, the Twin | _____ |
| ☐ John the Baptist Crossword Puzzle | _____ | ☐ Matthew, the Tax Collector | _____ |
| ☐ Jesus' Baptism and Mine | _____ | ☐ Same-Named Apostles | _____ |
| ☐ The Holy Spirit Like a Dove | _____ | ☐ Make a Pennant | _____ |
| ☐ Temptation Traps | _____ | ☐ Judas Iscariot, the Betrayer | _____ |
| ☐ Fight Back with the Word of God | _____ | ☐ Being Loyal to Jesus | _____ |
| ☐ Andrew | _____ | ☐ Who Am I? | _____ |
| ☐ Andrew, a Good Brother | _____ | ☐ Apostle Trivia Game | _____ |

# Answers—Jesus Is Born

**Page 8** The secret to having a great Christmas is to get to know Jesus.

| **Page 9** | **Page 14** | **Page 16** |
|---|---|---|
| 1-D | 1. Adam | Do not be <u>afraid</u>. You will give <u>birth</u> to a <u>son</u>, and you should name Him <u>Jesus</u>. The Holy One to be born will be the Son of <u>God</u>. |
| 2-B | 2. Jacob | |
| 3-C | 3. Abraham | |
| 4-F | 4. Solomon | |
| 5-A | 5. Mary | I am the Lord's <u>servant</u>. |
| 6-E | 6. Noah | |
| | 7. David | |

**Page 18**

Mary went to Judea to visit her cousin Elizabeth. Elizabeth and her husband, Zechariah, were expecting a baby, who would be John the Baptist.

As soon as Elizabeth heard Mary's voice, her baby jumped for joy inside her. Elizabeth called Mary "the mother of my Lord" and said, "You are blessed and so is your baby."

Mary praised God. She said, "My soul glorifies the Lord and my spirit rejoices in God my Savior. From now on all generations will call me blessed, for the Mighty One has done great things for me. Holy is His name."

**Page 19**

Taxes are money people pay to their country's leaders. Back in Bible times, people had to pay their taxes in person. To do this, Mary and Joseph traveled from their home town Nazareth in Galilee to Bethlehem in Judea. Mary was about to have a baby, but the inn where they stopped was full. So Mary had to give birth in a stable. She wrapped Jesus in strips of cloth called swaddling clothes and laid him in a manger (a box for animal food).

**Page 22**

The night Jesus was born, shepherds were watching their flocks. Suddenly a whole group of angels came to them and said, "Don't be afraid. We bring good news that will give great joy to all people. Today your Savior, Christ the Lord, was born in Bethlehem. You'll know you've found Him when you find a baby wrapped in swaddling clothes and lying in a manger."

The angels began praising God and saying "Glory to God in the highest. Peace and good will to all. "When the angels returned to heaven, the shepherds hurried and found Mary and Joseph and the baby.

Then the shepherds told everyone about the angels and the newborn baby. Mary remembered all these things and thought about them.

**Page 24**

```
D D O K A F O R D I A R F A E S T U
L S M D P N E Q T A D C B E B W F V
J Q V U B M I J O G D O N O T B Q R
R L B R G L D K M K G H F Y Z C H E
V J N B C H T S A U J W E M H D A Y
N Y O U R O P L R I X F L X G N I A
B S T W N J C D R V O N H I J D M D
B T N I B A I H Y M A R Y A E Z A O
T A R L C J G V U S G P R K L O P T
F E R L G I V E T Q X E W S B O R N
U T M F E D K B X I F O J A D B Y C
O O P N T M L I A B H G I W R Z U D
B Q R S Y O U R S A V I O R T S V O
P N V L W R Z T Y C F E K Y Q X W G
K G A M N O D H T O T H E S O N O F
```

**Page 28**

**Page 31**

THE WISE MEN MUST HAVE BEEN CLOSE TO GOD
TO KNOW THEY WERE SUPPOSED TO FOLLOW
THE STAR TO FIND JESUS. STAY CLOSE TO GOD
SO HE CAN GUIDE YOU.

# Answers—Jesus Grows Up

**Page 49**    1. Bethlehem; 2. Egypt; 3. Nazareth; 4. Jerusalem

**Page 50**    Swaddling - (3.) Clothes for wrapping a baby
Manger - (1.) Place where animal feed was kept
Stable - (2.) Place where animals were kept
Inn - (5.) Place for people to stay when they traveled
Tax - (4.) Money that was paid to the leaders of the country

**Page 51**    1. 4 B.C.; 2. 6 B.C.; 3. Answers vary depending on year of using book.

**Page 52**    When babies were born, parents had to take a sheep and a dove to the temple. If they were poor, they could bring two doves. It is likely that Joseph and Mary were poor because they brought a second dove and not a sheep.

**Page 53**    The Holy Spirit had told a man named Simeon that he would not die until he saw the person who would save the world. When he saw the baby Jesus, Simeon said, "Now, I can die in peace." He knew Jesus was the one who would save the world. A woman named Anna knew it, too. Do you know it?

**Page 54**    An <u>angel</u> appeared to <u>Joseph</u> in a <u>dream</u> and told him to take <u>Mary</u> and <u>Jesus</u> to <u>Egypt</u> and to stay there until the <u>angel</u> told him to bring them back. The <u>angel</u> said the cruel <u>king</u> would try to kill <u>Jesus</u>. <u>Joseph</u> obeyed.

Herod was probably afraid that <u>Jesus</u> would grow up and take his place on the <u>throne</u>. After <u>King</u> Herod died, <u>Joseph</u>, <u>Mary</u>, and <u>Jesus</u> moved to Nazareth in Galilee.

**Page 57**    1. Tunic; 2. Girdle; 3. Sandals; 4. Cloak; 5. Waistcloth

**Page 58**    1. Hallelujah; 2. Amen

**Page 59**    Jesus (ΙΗΣΟΥΣ) Christ (ΧΡΙΣΤΟΥ) God's (ΘΕΟΥ) Son (ΥΙΟΣ)
Savior (ΣΩΤΗΡ) ΙΧΘΥΣ

**Page 60**    Talent—$120,000; Aureus—$500; Stater—$60;
Didrachmon—$30; Drachma—$20; Assarion—$1;
Kodrantes—25¢; Lepton—$12\frac{1}{2}$¢

**Page 61**    1. Joseph; 2. Mary; 3. Jesus; 4. James; 5. Jude; 6. Joseph; 7. Simon

**Page 63**    1. God; 2. adopts; 3. Father

**Page 71**    The Passover was when Jewish people remembered the night God delivered them from slavery in Egypt. The people killed a lamb and put its blood on the doorposts. The angel passed over these homes and didn't kill anyone. Jesus called Himself the Passover lamb. His blood delivers us from sin and we can trust Christ to forgive us. He died on the cross for us so we can live forever in heaven someday.

**Page 72**   When God's people (Israelites) were freed from slavery in Egypt, they left too quickly to put leaven (what makes bread rise and become light) in the bread dough. After that, they had the Feast of Unleavened Bread each year.

During the feast they only ate flat, unleavened bread for a week and thanked God for taking them out of slavery.

**Page 77**

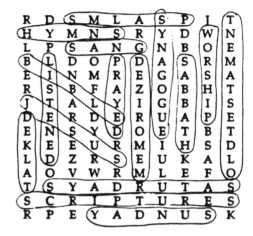

**Page 73**   The Holy Spirit

**Page 76**   Hear, O Israel: The Lord our God, the Lord is one. Love the Lord your God with all your heart and with all your soul and with all your strength.

**Page 78**   Every year Mary and Joseph went to Jerusalem for the Feast of the Passover.

When Jesus was twelve, He went with His family to Jerusalem. When they were returning to Nazareth, Mary and Joseph thought Jesus was with other people in their group. They traveled for a day and then began asking family and others if they knew where Jesus was. Mary and Joseph couldn't find Jesus, so they went back to Jerusalem to look for Him.

After three days they found Jesus in the temple with teachers all around Him. He was listening to them and asking questions. Everyone who heard Him was amazed by His understanding and answers.

Mary said, "Son, why have You treated us like this? Your father and I have been searching for You and have been very upset." Jesus said, "Why were you searching for Me? Didn't you want Me to be doing My Father's work?"

At the time, Mary and Joseph didn't understand that Jesus was talking about God the Father. But Mary remembered what Jesus had said.

**Page 79**   Jesus did not wait until He was grown to learn and serve His Father, God.

**Page 85**   LOVE THEM.

# Answers—Jesus Prepares to Serve

**Page 89**   Be like Jesus by listening to your teachers and asking questions about God.

**Page 90**   1. It teaches you what God is like.

2. It helps you know how God wants you to live.

3. It builds faith that Jesus saves whoever believes in Him.

**Page 91**   PREPARE

**Page 92**   Wild Honey

**Page 95**

**Page 99**   1. 2; 2. 1; 3. 3; 4. 2; 5. 1; 6. 3; 7. 3; 8. 3; 9. 2; 10. 3

**Page 101** 1-D; 2-A; 3-B; 4-C

**Page 102** 1. Read the Bible together.

2. Tell them ways that God answers your prayers.

3. Tell them when you are sorry so it is easier for them to forgive you.

4. Follow the golden rule and treat them as you want to be treated.

5. Show and tell them you love them.

6. Pray for them.

**Page 103** 1. net; 2. men; 3. hand; 4. water; 5. sink; 6. sun; 7. cloud; 8. fish; 9. girl; 10. keys; 11. throne; 12. twelve; 13. 77; 14. prison; 15. ear; 16. three; 17. rooster; 18. cried; 19. Bible

**Page 105** brothers, fishermen, mending, followed, fish, Thunder, face, Son, Revelation, mother

**Page 106** The apostle Jesus loved.

**Page 111**

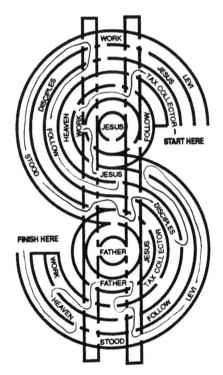

**Page 114** Judas Iscariot carried the money for the other apostles and Jesus. He often stole from the money bag.

Judas went to the Jewish leaders and made a deal with them to help them catch Jesus. They paid Judas thirty pieces of silver.

Judas told the Jewish leaders that he would let them know who Jesus was by kissing Him.

When Judas kissed Jesus in the Garden of Gethsemane, the Jewish leaders grabbed Jesus and took Him away.

**Page 116** 1. Nathanael; 2. James; 3. Andrew; 4. Thomas; 5. Judas Iscariot; 6. Peter; 7. John; 8. James; 9. Philip; 10. Matthew; 11. Judas; 12. Simon

# Index

## VOLUMES

**Volume 1**
**Jesus' Early Years**

Jesus Is Born

Jesus Grows Up

Jesus Prepares to Serve

**Volume 2**
**Jesus' Ministry**

Jesus Works Miracles

Jesus Heals

Jesus Teaches Me
to Pray

**Volume 3**
**Following Jesus**

Names of Jesus

Following Jesus

Learning to Love
Like Jesus

**Volume 4**
**The Love of Jesus**

Jesus Shows God's Love

Jesus' Last Week

Jesus Is Alive!

| BIBLE STORY | LIFE AND LESSONS | BIBLE STORY | LIFE AND LESSONS |
|---|---|---|---|
| Healing of: | | Jesus Is: | |
| 10 Lepers | Vol. 2 | the Light | Vol. 3 |
| Blind Man | Vol. 3 | the Redeemer | Vol. 3 |
| Deaf and Mute Man | Vol. 3 | the Resurrection and Life | Vol. 3 |
| A Leper | Vol. 2 | the Savior | Vol. 3 |
| A Man's Hand | Vol. 2 | the Son of God | Vol. 3 |
| Blind Bartimaeus | Vol. 2 | the Truth | Vol. 3 |
| Centurion's Servant | Vol. 2 | the Vine | Vol. 3 |
| Epileptic Boy | Vol. 2 | the Way | Vols. 3, 4 |
| Malchus's Ear | Vol. 2 | the Word | Vol. 3 |
| Man Born Blind | Vol. 3 | Jesus Loves Children | Vol. 4 |
| Man with Dropsy | Vol. 2 | Jesus Obeys Parents | Vol. 1 |
| Official's Son | Vol. 2 | Jesus Prayed | Vol. 2 |
| Peter's Mother-in-Law | Vol. 2 | Jesus Shows Compassion | Vol. 4 |
| Paralytic | Vol. 2 | Jesus Washes Disciples' Feet | Vols. 3, 4 |
| Woman's Back | Vol. 2 | Jesus' Family | Vol. 1 |
| Woman Who Touched Hem | Vol. 2 | Jesus' Genealogy | Vol. 1 |
| Heaven | Vol. 4 | Jesus' Trial Before Caiaphas | Vol. 4 |
| How Much God Loves Us | Vol. 4 | Jesus' Trial Before Pilate | Vol. 4 |
| Humble Prayer | Vol. 2 | John the Baptist | Vol. 1 |
| **I** | | Joseph's Dream | Vol. 1 |
| I Am with You Always | Vol. 4 | Judas Betrays Jesus | Vols. 1, 4 |
| I Live/You Will Live | Vol. 4 | Judge Not | Vol. 3 |
| Include Others | Vol. 3 | **K** | |
| **J** | | Known by Fruits | Vol. 3 |
| Jesus Clears the Temple | Vol. 4 | **L** | |
| Jesus Died for Me | Vol. 4 | Last Supper | Vol. 4 |
| Jesus Eats with Sinners | Vol. 4 | Lay Down Life for Friends | Vols. 3, 4 |
| Jesus Has Overcome the World | Vol. 4 | Lazarus and the Rich Man | Vol. 3 |
| Jesus Is: | | Life in New Testament Times | Vol. 1 |
| 'I AM' | Vol. 3 | Light on a Hill | Vol. 3 |
| Arrested | Vol. 4 | Like Days of Noah | Vol. 4 |
| Born | Vol. 1 | Like Jonah's Three Days in Fish | Vol. 4 |
| Buried | Vol. 4 | Lord's Prayer | Vol. 2 |
| Christ | Vols. 1, 3 | Love Each Other | Vol. 4 |
| Crucified and Dies | Vol. 4 | Love Jesus Most | Vol. 4 |
| God | Vol. 3 | Love Me/Obey Me | Vol. 4 |
| Immanuel | Vol. 3 | Love One Another | Vol. 3 |
| Tempted | Vol. 1 | Loving Enemies | Vols. 2, 3 |
| the Bread of Life | Vol. 3 | **M** | |
| the Bridegroom | Vol. 3 | Make Up Quickly | Vol. 3 |
| the Chief Cornerstone | Vol. 3 | Maps of New Testament Times | Vols. 1, 2 |
| the Gate | Vol. 3 | Mary and Martha | Vol. 3 |
| the Gift of God | Vol. 3 | Mary Anoints Jesus with Perfume | Vol. 4 |
| the Good Shepherd | Vol. 3 | Mary Visits Elizabeth | Vol. 1 |
| the Lamb of God | Vol. 3 | | |